COUPLING
Strategies for Infrastructural Opportunism

PAMPHLET ARCHITECTURE 30
INFRANET LAB / LATERAL OFFICE
Neeraj Bhatia / Maya Przybylski / Lola Sheppard / Mason White

Princeton Architectural Press, New York

Published by
Princeton Architectural Press
37 East Seventh Street
New York, New York 10003

For a free catalog of books, call 1.800.722.6657.
Visit our website at www.papress.com.

© 2011 Princeton Architectural Press
All rights reserved
Printed and bound in Canada by Friesens
14 13 12 11 4 3 2 1 First edition

NATIONAL
ENDOWMENT
FOR THE ARTS

This project is supported in part by an award from the National Endowment
for the Arts.

Editor: Becca Casbon
Designer: Fei-Ling Tseng / InfraNet Lab

Special thanks to: Bree Anne Apperley, Sara Bader, Nicola Bednarek Brower,
Janet Behning, Megan Carey, Carina Cha, Tom Cho, Penny (Yuen Pik) Chu,
Russell Fernandez, Pete Fitzpatrick, Jan Haux, Linda Lee, John Myers, Katharine
Myers, Margaret Rogalski, Dan Simon, Andrew Stepanian, Jennifer Thompson,
Paul Wagner, Joseph Weston, and Deb Wood of Princeton Architectural Press
—Kevin C. Lippert, publisher

Library of Congress Cataloging-in-Publication Data
Pamphlet architecture 30 : coupling : strategies for infrastructural opportunism /
InfraNet Lab/Lateral Office, Neeraj Bhatia ... [et al.]. -- 1st ed.
    p. cm.
Includes bibliographical references and index.
ISBN 978-1-56898-985-3 (alk. paper)
1. Architecture--Environmental aspects. 2. Infrastructure (Economics)--Planning.
3. Engineering design. I. Bhatia, Neeraj. II. InfraNet Lab (Firm) III. Lateral Office
(Firm) IV. Title: Pamphlet architecture thirty. V. Title: Coupling : strategies for infra-
structural opportunism.
NA2542.35.P36 2010
724'.7--dc22
                        2010043984

Airport

Roads

Highways

Railway

High Speed Rail

Trucking

Ports

Shipping

Bridges

Tunnels

Pipelines

Wind Energy

Geothermal Energy

Drinking Water

Internet

Submarine Cables

Server Farms

Landfills

Greenhouses

Agriculture

Buoys

2500 BC | 2000 | 1500 | 1000 | 500 BC | 0 | 500 AD | 1000 | 1500 | 1600 | 1700 | 1800 | 1900 | 1910 | 1920 | 1930 | 1940 | 1950 | 1960 | 1970 | 1980 | 1990 | 2000

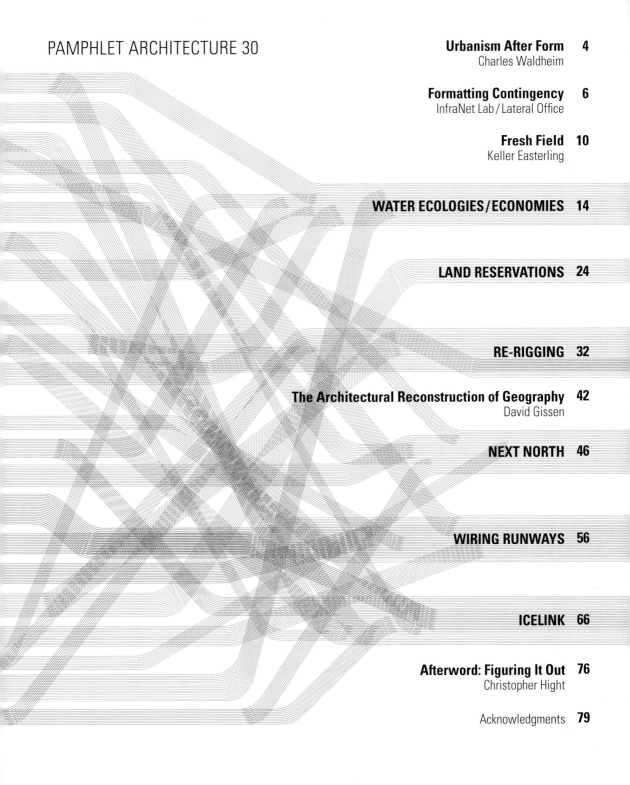

PAMPHLET ARCHITECTURE 30

URBANISM AFTER FORM

Charles Waldheim

This publication and the work of InfraNet Lab/Lateral Office document the postmodern co-option of architecture as a metaphor signifying complexity and synthesis in systems associated with business and information. Through the re-appropriation of architecture in its metaphoric sense, the authors re-imagine the disciplinary and professional commitments of "capital A" Architecture to include the traditional externalities of social, environmental, and various other mediated contents. In so doing, InfraNet Lab/Lateral Office mobilizes infrastructure as site and subject of their opening up of architecture to previously external conditions. Through infrastructure, InfraNet Lab/Lateral Office seeks to reanimate architectural discourse with urban (read: social and environmental) relevance. Equally, they seek to capture a broader audience for architectural production, aspiring to move the field from its cultural confines into the more quotidian qualities of daily life.

In this aspiration, InfraNet Lab/Lateral Office is not alone. Through this work, and the publication of this pamphlet, the authors propose themselves for membership in a distinct genealogy of architects *cum* urbanists who see infrastructure as a means to reconciling architecture's contemporary potential with its historic relationship to the city. For the past two generations (at least), architects involved with the urban have identified infrastructure as a privileged way forward. This has had much to do with the fact that urban infrastructure has been repositioned as a topic combining the potential for social and environmental progress, while avoiding the blind alleys and dark corners of urban form.

By postponing the question of urban form, proponents of an infrastructural approach to the architecture of the city suggest that a focus on performance criteria, operational imperatives, and contemporary flows might allow us to reengage with social and environmental subjects without participating in the culture wars of the past. In this family tree, one would comfortably place the previous generation of postmodern urbanists, particularly those trained in Europe with a taste for American theory (Koolhaas, Wall, Mostafavi, Zaero-Polo, Corner, et al.). For those, and others, infrastructure emerged as a topic with traction as it afforded an instrumental and operational way forward for urbanization, while avoiding what had become the twin cul-de-sacs of historicism and typology.

By postponing questions of form, the putative avant-garde architect urbanist of the late 1970s and 1980s (not to say 1990s and 2000s) could reengage the aspirations of the modern project, while maintaining a position of ambivalence regarding the neo-liberal flows of globalization. This position proved prescient, as it has emerged among the most durable strains of discourse on urban topics for over a quarter century. To this historical project, InfraNet Lab / Lateral Office has added a nimble programmatic array and an abiding concern for ecological contexts, inputs, and outcomes. More recently, that discourse has been reabsorbed into contemporary debates around urban design, planning, and landscape architecture. For the urban arts, infrastructure has signified a myth of eternal return, wherein planners and urban designers might regain lost market share and relevance. For landscape architects (and landscape urbanists), a focus on infrastructure promised to return the field to its historic sense of centrality, and as a riposte to civil engineering's imperious attitude toward the subject. Most recently, this line of work has informed the emergent understandings of landscape infrastructure and ecological urbanism.

Notwithstanding the historic and contemporary merits of such a project, the work of InfraNet Lab / Lateral Office presented here avoids the clichéd naiveté of much that stands for an infrastructural approach to urbanism today. In so doing, the work demands further consideration, and reminds the attentive reader of many under-pursued potentials in the infrastructural approach to urbanism yet to be explored.

Charles Waldheim is John E. Irving Professor and Chair of Landscape Architecture at Harvard University Graduate School of Design.

FORMATTING CONTINGENCY

InfraNet Lab / Lateral Office

These are things we do not know we don't know.
—Donald Rumsfeld, February 12, 2002

Any environmental design task is characterized by an astounding amount of unavailable or indeterminate information.
—Nicholas Negroponte, *The Architecture Machine*

Co-optings

Computation and business theory both co-opted a strand of meaning from the term "architecture" in the 1960s to seed a radical repositioning within their respective fields. "Architecture" was used as a suffix, signifying at once organizational complexity and networked wholeness. It could be argued that from this moment, the term "architecture" and the discipline of architecture began evolving along separate routes. "Business architecture" and "information architecture," for example, adopted an architectural idiom to signify their complex economic conditions and expanded data fields, today understood to be spurred by globalizing forces. As the word took on varied meanings, it further came to signify—outside of its discipline proper—a dynamic superorganism, capable of processing disparate extrinsic matter.[1] Systems thinking had also migrated into architecture through the megastructure movement of buildings as city systems, which reached a fever pitch in the late 1960s. However, this early systems architecture typically focused on the internal systems of the architectural object, and failed to acknowledge the systems of environment that envelop architecture. The year 1967 was witness to two notable co-optings of the term architecture as a system: Nicholas Negroponte's initiation of the Architecture Machine Group, the precursor of the MIT Media Lab, and the publishing of economists Paul R. Lawrence and Jay W. Lorsch's landmark book, *Organization and Environment: Managing Differentiation and Integration.*

Coupling: Strategies for Infrastructural Opportunism presents a body of work that seeks to reintegrate architecture as a systems-based organization, as an activity within the broader globalized exchanges of economics, data, ecologies, politics, and land use—architecture after the superorganism. The work explores the possibilities of how architecture might benefit from a reintroduction of the term "architecture," as it has evolved within business, management, computation, and information architecture practices. From this reintroduction, architecture has the capacity to operate as a dynamic infrastructure within an increasingly complex and intertwined environment.

Architecture After Contingency

Lawrence and Lorsch were both professors of organizational behavior at Harvard Business School at the time *Organization and Environment* was published in 1967. The authors criticized the then-common organization theory for ignoring "relationships between the structural characteristics of complex organizations and the environmental conditions these organizations face."[2] In contrast, they sought an organization architecture that was more responsive to factors from extrinsic forces, or the wider environment. Extracting the unpredictability of the extrinsic from the more predictable intrinsic factors, Lawrence and Lorsch proposed a contingency theory of organization. From this viewpoint, external contingencies were considered to be constraints as well as opportunities that internal structures and processes responded to. At its root, contingency theory suggests that managers should no longer privilege "one best way" to organize. Given this, it follows that organization architecture should anticipate inevitable change. As competing methodologies of contingency planning emerged throughout the 1960s and 1970s, systems thinking expanded to include the idea of an open system, which continuously interacts with and adapts to its environment. In the natural sciences, an open system is permeable to both energy and mass. Military and disaster protocols fully embraced contingency planning, to the point that a National Contingency Plan was devised in 1968 to anticipate hazardous substance releases, such as oil spills.

The year 1967 also saw the establishment of the Architecture Machine Group at MIT. Negroponte considered any design act to also be an act of procuring information, and thereby declared that the group would be dedicated to "the construction of a machine that can work with missing information."[3] Managing contingencies that arose from problems of missing information presented a rather different set of challenges in architecture. Negroponte was mainly interested in architect-machine symbiosis, and in a fluid discourse between the interface with machines, architects would not need to be computation specialists. Artist Peggy Weil, an early collaborator with the Architecture Machine Group, observed that her work took place "in an atmosphere of complete improvisation: using machines and tools for reasons far afield from their original applications."[4] While Negroponte's group primarily focused on establishing a hybrid process that embraced a machine as

an equal associate in the design process, the group's ambition of establishing a machine process that could work with unavailable or missing information could be said to echo the contingencies associated with open-system thinking. This suggested that data was neither an absolute nor a static framework from which to respond; information was as much a living system as any other. An array of architecture-termed pursuits subsequently flourished: enterprise architecture, data architecture, application architecture, and information architecture, among others.

The term "architecture" as employed in the above examples catalyzed a shift from what might be called a command-and-control organization to an approach approximating real-time responsive organization—the transition from architecture as a static, hierarchical enterprise to it operating as a dynamic element, interacting within, and at times structuring, networks. With newfound vigor, the term introduced contingency into disciplines whose very foundations were predominantly procedural. Could this be recuperated into architecture, the discipline?

Contingency, as with design, is an anticipatory act, and is often devised as a response to an eventuality. Contingency triggers the recuperation of an extrinsic architecture. The role of contingency in architecture permits opportunism at the moment when architecture interacts with the complexity of its wider environment—an environment often possessing characteristics of a superorganism. As with living organisms, the performance of any organization depends on the alignment and adaptability between the system and its environment. The filtering and selection of data from inevitably inadequate information sets, as Negroponte suggests, combined with Lawrence and Lorsch's observation of "contingencies as opportunities," is central to the intentions of the work included in *Coupling*. In the book, we ask: After the term "architecture" is absorbed back into the profession of architecture, what kind of architecture results?

Formats: Surfaces, Containers, and Conduits

Designing for contingency has no prescribed methodology in architecture, though certainly all architecture is already charged with anticipating possible eventualities— higher loading, inclement weather, potential of fire, or even change of use. However, anticipated contingencies typically focus on mitigation rather than opportunism. And an architecture that responds to opportunities of contingency is manifest in atypical spatial formats. Performing in a manner similar to infrastructures, these spatial formats support energies, flows, resources, and matter, yielding an emergent multivalent public realm. *Coupling* identifies three spatial formats in which a contingent architecture might materialize: surfaces, containers, and conduits. Each format mediates between architecture and its environment, between the biological and the infrastructural, the entrepreneurial and the logical—simultaneously performing the roles of both. These formats enjoy an ignorance of

the prejudices that distinguish architecture from infrastructure, landscape, and urbanism—instead relishing the dynamic ambiguity of a spatial format, or "spatial product."[5]

Much as Rosalind Krauss positioned and qualified sculpture practices in her essay "Sculpture and the Expanded Field" some thirty years ago, so too should infrastructure be qualified in an expanded field today.[6] Using a Klein group diagram, Krauss identified three subpractices of sculpture that had previously been buried within a generalization of sculpture. She qualifies them as "site-construction," "marked sites," and "axiomatic structures." These three uncovered practices became disciplinary parallels to sculptural practices. Today, architecture—previously absorbed within Krauss's group—is in need of qualifiers to establish its position among the expanding disciplinary terrain of landscape architecture and urbanism. Toward this end, we suggest removing architecture from the original group and replacing it with urbanism, which is missing from Krauss's original diagram. From this new group we identify three subpractices of architecture from infrastructure's expanded field: productive surfaces, programmed containers, and civic conduits. Identifying infrastructure in the expanded field reveals new formats and operations for architecture as a conduit, container, and surface within the capacities of infrastructure.

What are these formats? Surfaces are planes of mediation, thickened and intelligent. Containers are shells of enclosure, processing and performing as nodes within a network. Conduits are carriers of matter and energy, exchanging and transferring within a larger network. Formats suggest an emergent productive public realm, one in which performative processes are integral to occupation. Rather than each operating as a single format, the projects in *Coupling* exhibit varying combinations of formats: conduits lined with containers (IceLink), resurfaced containers networked by conduits (Land Reservations), or containers lined with intersecting surfaces (Wiring Runways). While one format typically serves as the primary organizational device, other formats absorb contingencies or account for missing information. The projects and proposals take the position that infrastructures operate as contingent ecologies, or managed dynamic systems. Identifying their role and how they interrelate becomes an act of design coupling.

Coupling

The twentieth century was witness to both an infrastructure boom and bust. It is the twenty-first century that will need to determine not only how to address crumbling and ineffective infrastructure, but also how to position new infrastructures that confront urgent issues of climate change, sustenance inequality, and environment degradation. The opportunity for projecting a future infrastructure lies in bundling multiple processes with spatial experiences. The work in this book aims to declare infrastructures as open systems, adaptive and responsive to environments and occupation.

Coupling employs interventions that also operate extrinsically, sometimes at a territorial scale. Easily replaced or upgraded, these infrastructures double as landscape life support, creating new sites for production and recreation. The ambition is to supplement ecologies at risk rather than overhaul them. The following six design/research projects merge landscape, urbanism, and architecture into a mutant assemblage of surfaces, containers, and conduits. Existing landscapes meld with emergent systems to catalyze a multivalent network for a new public realm. Seeking opportunistic associations between economy, ecology, politics, and information, coupling is not simply a combinatory exercise so much as a typological investigation into new spatial formats for the twenty-first century.

1. Although much of the theory of superorganisms is centered on the eusocial behavior of organisms, as best chronicled by sociobiologists Bert Hölldobler and E. O. Wilson in *The Superorganism* (New York: W. W. Norton & Company, 2009), we use the term here to suggest a highly interconnected set of environments, as well as the occupants of these environments.

2. Paul R. Lawrence and Jay W. Lorsch, *Organization and Environment: Managing Differentiation and Integration* (Boston: Harvard Business Press, 1967), v.

3. Nicholas Negroponte, *The Architecture Machine* (Cambridge, MA: The MIT Press, 1970), 119.

4. Accessed from http://www.lnkall.com/projects/archmacprojects.html on June 18, 2010.

5. Keller Easterling uses the term "spatial product" in reference to how the market uses the phrase "real estate product." Both suggest formulas for space prior to realization and construction.

6. See Rosalind Krauss, "Sculpture in the Expanded Field," *October* 8 (Spring 1979): 30–44.

While infrastructure typically conjures associations with physical networks for transportation, communication, or utilities, it also includes the countless shared protocols that format everything from technical objects to management styles to the spaces of urbanism—defining the world as it is clasped and engaged in the space of everyday life. Infrastructural space is, as the word suggests, customarily regarded as a hidden substrate—the binding medium or current between objects of positive consequence, shape, and law—yet it is also the point of contact and access, the spatial outcropping of underlying laws and logics. However invisible they are, the microwaves that bounce from satellites or the thickening tangles of fiber-optic submarine cable that lie on the bottom of the ocean nevertheless materialize in atomized swarms of ubiquitous electronic devices. Moreover, some infrastructural formulations seem to make manifest and press into view a hyperbolic cartoon of their abstract technical and economic logics. Traffic engineering formulas dictate that tiny houses in suburbia be set back sixty feet from a street that is equally wide. Repeatable formulas for spatial products like resorts, malls, IT campuses, or free zones are manifest in gigantic world city formations. The building enclosures typically considered to be geometric formal objects have become infrastructural—physical, spatial media

and technologies moving around the world as repeatable phenomena. No longer simply what is hidden or beneath another urban structure, many infrastructures are the urban formula, the very parameters of global urbanism.

Some of the most radical changes to the globalizing world are being written not in the language of law and diplomacy, but rather in a spatial language of infrastructure, architecture, and urbanism. These mixtures of spatial hardware and software are capable of generating new forms of polity faster than official forms of governance can legislate them. Whether suppressed, ubiquitous, or tangible, on an international scale the forces that determine credit card thicknesses, microwave densities, or submarine cable locations are obscure and distanced from more familiar legislative processes, and are resistant to social and economic sciences. Massive global infrastructure systems, administered by mixtures of public and private cohorts and driven by profound irrationalities, form a wilder mongrel than any storied leviathan for which there is a studied political response.

The space of global infrastructure is, then, a fresh field—a new pasture of territory and opportunity that lies on the other side of an altered theoretical framework. The seemingly

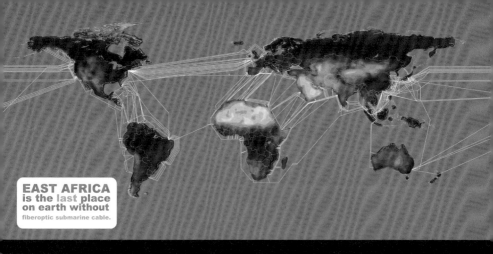

EAST AFRICA is the last place on earth without fiberoptic submarine cable.

CABLE: Three cables have recently landed in East Africa, the last place on earth to receive an international fiber-optic connection.

nnocuous layers of infrastructural space are filled with profound indicators about how the world really works, but they also tutor special artistic and political faculties. When making infrastructure or infrastructural architecture, one is not only shaping outlines and profiles, but also agency and disposition. As InfraNet Lab / Lateral Office note, the sciences as well as the arts have explored their "architecture," or matrix space—their infinitive as well as their nominative expressions for form. Architects, however, rarely train to make action, and spaces are rarely considered to possess dispositions. Buildings, landscapes, or volumes are usually treated as objects or compositions with appearances, geometrical profiles, or visual patterns, not as actors with agency or temperament immanent to their arrangement.

Disposition, as it is used in philosophy, art, and even common parlance, usually describes an unfolding understanding of capacity or relative

ball on an inclined plane possesses disposition, and it need not roll down the hill to retain that capacity. Disposition locates activity not in movement or event, but in relationship or relative position. It cannot be named, but rather remains as a latent or serialized propensity or property. To use philosopher Gilbert Ryle's distinction, an understanding of disposition must overcome the mind's stubborn foregrounding of name and specific event over action. Understanding disposition involves "knowing how," not "knowing that."[1]

Infrastructure is dispositional, and as a composition of action rather than geometry it redoubles our form-making capacities. The dispositional composition of infrastructure is conditioned and inflected with active forms— spatial agents or actors that shape not only the object, but the way the object plays. They condition material and immaterial parameters, aesthetic practices, and political trajectories.

way that some alteration performs within a group, multiplies across a field, reconditions a population, or generates a network. They may be not only physical objects or contagion, but also topologies or organizational properties within a spatial field. The designer of active forms is creating the delta, or the means by which the organization changes—not the field in its entirety, but the way that field is inflected. So while perhaps intensely involved with material and geometry, active forms are inclusive of but not limited to enclosure, and may move beyond the conventional architectural site. An active form is not at odds with, but rather propels and expands (even rescues) form as an object. As they may ride larger organizations, they offer additional modes of authorship with time-released powers and cascading effects.

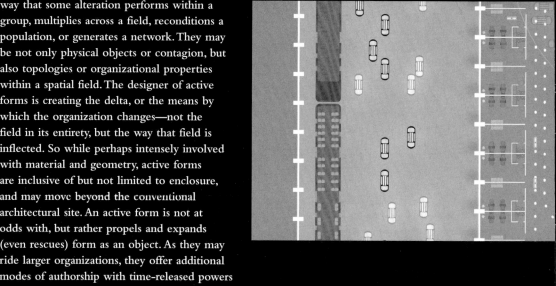

The environment grows or changes because of active forms within it—an elevator, spatial product, law, real estate wrinkle, financial formula, network topology, material imperative, or persuasion. Like the surfaces, containers, and conduits that are active in the projects of this pamphlet, the forms are carriers of both geometry and protocol. They contribute deliberate tools for adjusting organizational constitution to render mixtures that are, for instance, homogenous, heterogeneous, monopolistic, oligarchic, open, resilient, or recursive.

The fresh field of infrastructure also opens onto an expanded political repertoire. The most powerful players have the capacity to make infrastructure, but equally important, infrastructure can escape nominative designations or documented events. As an action, it can remain undeclared and discrepant, and as a medium, it can determine what survives. Different from political tactics that name and square off against every opponent, as if to kill every weed in the field, the indeterminate dispositional space of infrastructure may neutralize or adjust by changing the chemistry of the soil. The broad foundational transformations of infrastructural modifications—like sea changes or changes to an operating system—offer a special political instrumentality that may preclude the fight. While political traditions that call for inversions and revolutions often call for the absolute annihilation of the preceding system, lateral techniques of dissensus work on the *ongoing* reconditioning of a spatio-political climate.

The action is the form.

1. Gilbert Ryle, *The Concept of Mind* (Chicago: University of Chicago Press, 1984).

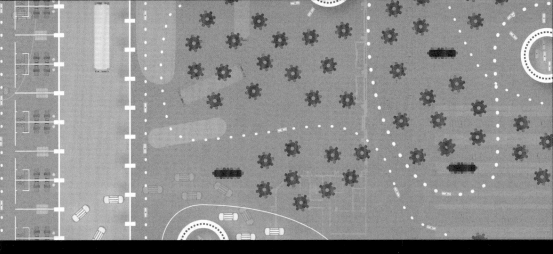

FLOOR: Now the script for a fleet of new conveyance vehicles, the ordinary floor is quickly becoming the most important architectural surface.

WATER ECOLOGIES/
ECONOMIES

An increasingly saline terminal lake in
California is resuscitated as a water farm,
recreational retreat, and habitat haven.

WATER ECOLOGIES / ECONOMIES: FARMING A TERMINAL LAKE

Salton Sea, California, United States 33°15' N, 115°42' W

Perhaps the most striking aspect of the water infrastructure sustaining the American Southwest is the accelerated rate at which landscapes and ecologies are created, erased, and redefined. An extreme example is the Salton Sea in California, formed in 1905 during a season of heavy rain that caused the Colorado River to breach its canal, flooding the Imperial Valley and refilling an ancient inland seabed. The Salton is endorheic, or terminal, and has high evaporation rates. Officially designated as an agricultural sump for the massive farming operations of the Imperial Valley, its highly salinated water levels are perpetuated by agricultural runoff.

The Salton Sea's extreme salinity and threatened ecosystems offer an opportunity for economic, social, and ecological innovations. This proposal establishes the sea as a unique site for water harvesting. No longer serving as a hydrological sump or supporting a mono-agricultural landscape, the Salton would offer new forms of leisure, protected habitats, and industries—harvesting

fish, kelp, water, and (in a return to its namesake) salt. The proposal offers three zones of coastal development: an ecology zone, an industry zone, and a recreational zone. Floating pools, or water-pads, of various sizes and salinities serve as salinity-regulation devices as well as harvest plots, habitats, and recreational destinations. The pool types vary in dimension, complexity, depth (to control evaporation rates), and width (to suggest different uses). Pools aggregate to establish intensified habitats or harvests. Acting as micro-ecologies, they can be partially moored in place or migrate within a territorial range of the Salton Sea.

Regulating the water's salinity levels, saltwater pools separate salt from freshwater through passive solar desalination, where freshwater condenses on a transparent fabric and collects in the hollow structural ring of each pool. Briny by-products foster high-salinity habitats. Meanwhile, salt is harvested, shifting a current ecological liability into an economic and environmental asset.

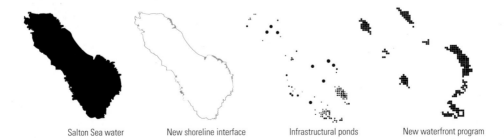

| Salton Sea water | New shoreline interface | Infrastructural ponds | New waterfront program |

Coachella

Salton Sea State Recreational Area
Headquarters and Visitor Center Campground

AQUACULTURE
Las Vegas, CA - 315km
Phoenix, AZ - 350km
Albuquerque, NM - 868km

WATER EXPORT
to nearby large cities
San Diego, CA - 140km - pop. 1,223,400
Los Angeles, CA - 235km - pop. 3,694,820
Las Vegas, CA - 315km - pop. 1,865,746

SALT EXPORT
to Canada

Coachella Canal

Salton Sea

Imperial Hot
Mineral Spa
and RV Park

Salton City

Salton Sea
Naval Test Range

TOURISM
LAX 235 km
FK 3770 km
MS 8905 km

LEISURE ECONOMY
Mexicali 85km
San Diego 140km
Las Vegas 315km

BIRD SANCTUARY
~1,000,000 birds annually
attracting birdwatchers
and researchers

San Felipe Creek

Pacific Flyway Route

Imperial Valley

SALT EXPORT
to Mexico

New River

2010

2025

Productive Ecologies
Reactivating the Salton Sea from an
aqueous sump to economically
productive territory

Sea as water dump

Sea as waterfront

17

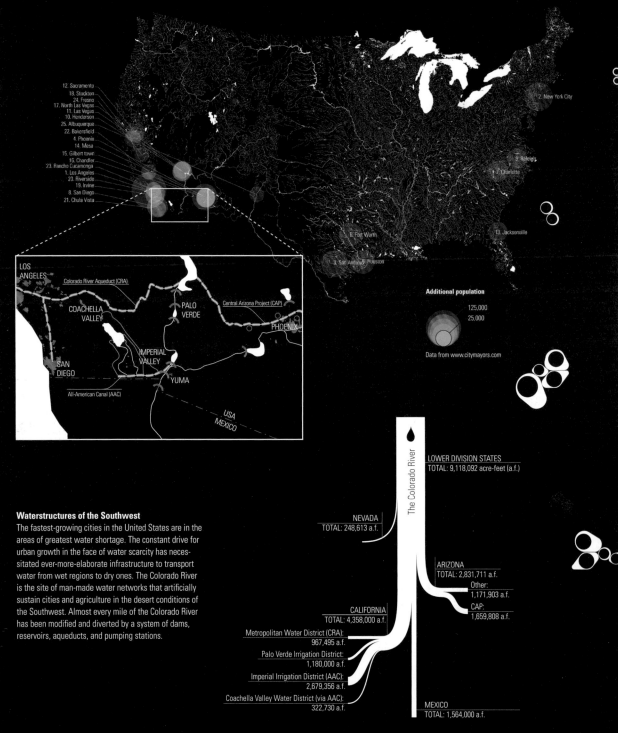

12. Sacramento
18. Stockton
24. Fresno
17. North Las Vegas
11. Las Vegas
10. Henderson
25. Albuquerque
22. Bakersfield
4. Phoenix
14. Mesa
15. Gilbert town
16. Chandler
23. Rancho Cucamonga
1. Los Angeles
20. Riverside
19. Irvine
8. San Diego
21. Chula Vista

2. New York City

9. Raleigh
7. Charlotte

6. Fort Worth

13. Jacksonville

3. San Antonio 5. Houston

LOS ANGELES
Colorado River Aqueduct (CRA)
COACHELLA VALLEY
PALO VERDE
Central Arizona Project (CAP)
PHOENIX
IMPERIAL VALLEY
SAN DIEGO
YUMA
All-American Canal (AAC)
USA
MEXICO

Additional population

125,000

25,000

Data from www.citymayors.com

Waterstructures of the Southwest

The fastest-growing cities in the United States are in the areas of greatest water shortage. The constant drive for urban growth in the face of water scarcity has necessitated ever-more-elaborate infrastructure to transport water from wet regions to dry ones. The Colorado River is the site of man-made water networks that artificially sustain cities and agriculture in the desert conditions of the Southwest. Almost every mile of the Colorado River has been modified and diverted by a system of dams, reservoirs, aqueducts, and pumping stations.

The Colorado River

LOWER DIVISION STATES
TOTAL: 9,118,092 acre-feet (a.f.)

NEVADA
TOTAL: 248,613 a.f.

ARIZONA
TOTAL: 2,831,711 a.f.
Other:
1,171,903 a.f.
CAP:
1,659,808 a.f.

CALIFORNIA
TOTAL: 4,358,000 a.f.
Metropolitan Water District (CRA):
967,495 a.f.
Palo Verde Irrigation District:
1,180,000 a.f.
Imperial Irrigation District (AAC):
2,679,356 a.f.
Coachella Valley Water District (via AAC):
322,730 a.f.

MEXICO
TOTAL: 1,564,000 a.f.

Allocating the Colorado River's Flow
Data from the 2009 Colorado River Accounting and Water Use Report

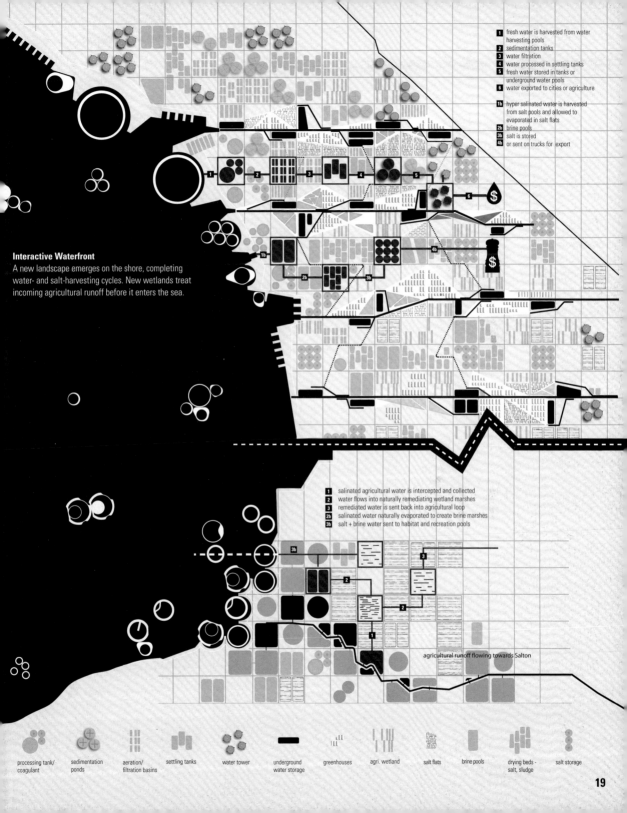

Interactive Waterfront

A new landscape emerges on the shore, completing
water- and salt-harvesting cycles. New wetlands treat
incoming agricultural runoff before it enters the sea.

1 fresh water is harvested from water harvesting pools
2 sedimentation tanks
3 water filtration
4 water processed in settling tanks
5 fresh water stored in tanks or underground water pools
6 water exported to cities or agriculture

1b hyper salinated water is harvested from salt pools and allowed to evaporated in salt flats
2b brine pools
3b salt is stored
4b or sent on trucks for export

1 salinated agricultural water is intercepted and collected
2 water flows into naturally remediating wetland marshes
3 remediated water is sent back into agricultural loop
2b salinated water naturally evaporated to create brine marshes
3b salt + brine water sent to habitat and recreation pools

agricultural runoff flowing towards Salton

processing tank/ coagulant   sedimentation ponds   aeration/ filtration basins   settling tanks   water tower   underground water storage   greenhouses   agri. wetland   salt flats   brine pools   drying beds - salt, sludge   salt storage

Aquaculture/Kelp: Cluster

1. Salt harvester and algae nursery feed brine shrimp
2. Brine shrimp feed fish culture
3. Fish culture waste is cleaned by kelp nursery
4. Kelp is brought onto pool platforms to dry in sun
5. Fish and kelp are brought to shore for harvest

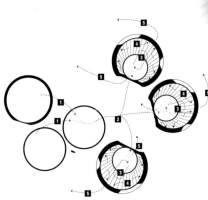

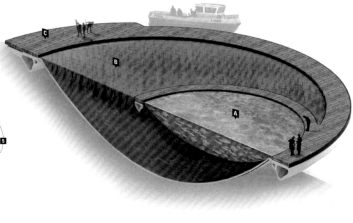

Aquaculture/Kelp: Operation
A. Fish farm
B. Kelp farm
C. Kelp drying platform

Habitat: Cluster

1. Salton Sea is a major bird migratory area
2. Habitat mass is created by clustering of pools
3. Brine shrimp and algae pools provide food for birds

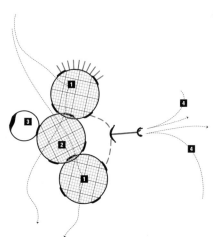

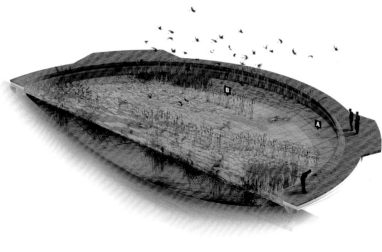

Habitat: Occupation
A. Mesh of suspended growth media
B. Wetland vegetation

20

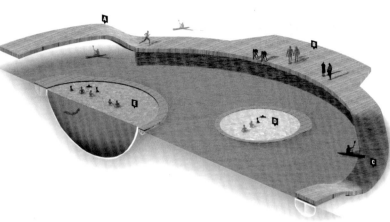

Recreation: Cluster
1. Boats pull up to recreation pool
2. Freshwater pools deliver recreation pool
3. Saltwater feeds therapeutic pools

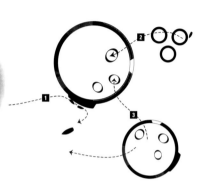

Recreation: Occupation
A. Diving platforms
B. Tanning decks
C. Marina
D. Freshwater pool
E. Hypersaline pool

Salt/Water: Cluster
1. Water pool takes in saline sea water
2. Desalinated water delivered to shore for treatment
3. Brine pools deliver saltwater for salt harvesting

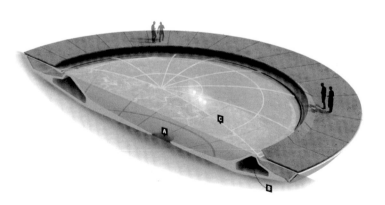

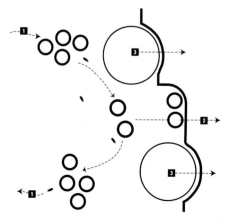

Salt/Water: Operation
A. Saltwater intake
B. Freshwater harvesting
C. Evaporation/condensation dome

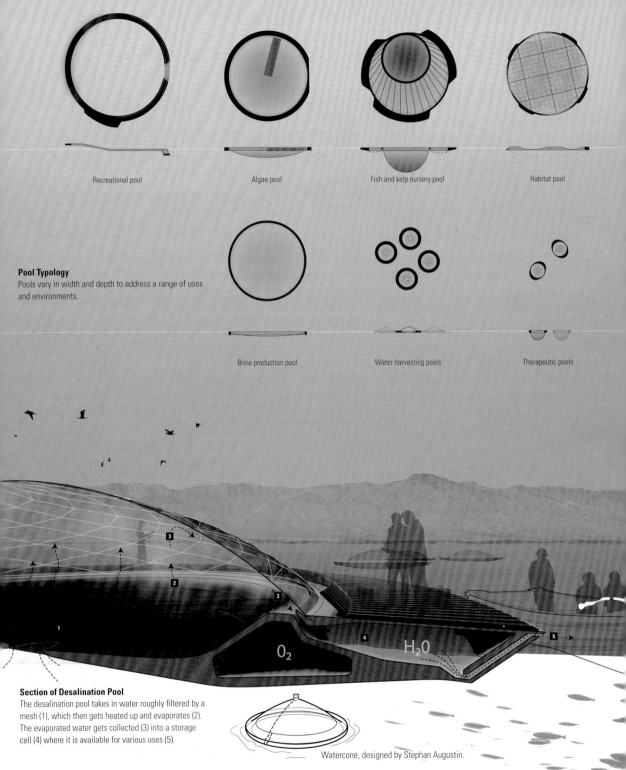

Recreational pool

Algae pool

Fish and kelp nursery pool

Habitat pool

Pool Typology
Pools vary in width and depth to address a range of uses and environments.

Brine production pool

Water harvesting pools

Therapeutic pools

O₂

H₂O

Section of Desalination Pool
The desalination pool takes in water roughly filtered by a mesh (1), which then gets heated up and evaporates (2). The evaporated water gets collected (3) into a storage cell (4) where it is available for various uses (5).

Watercone, designed by Stephan Augustin.

Pools for Hybrid Ecologies
View of ecology delta, with remediating wetlands treating the agricultural runoff of the Imperial Valley before entering the Salton Sea

Pools for Salt Farming
View of industry waterfront with large water harvester brought to shore

Pools for Recreation
View of new recreation waterfront with pools and expanded shoreline in Salton City

LANDFILL REGULATION
WETLAND MITIGATION
SOLID WASTE IMPACTS
PLACEMENT
CONSTRUCTION
LANDFILLS
SUBTITLE-D

MI-EPA
MICHIGAN
US-EPA
U.S.A.
NAFTA — INTERNATIONAL

FERTILIZERS ACT

TRANSPORTATION OF DANGEROUS GOODS ACT
ENVIRONMENTAL ASSESSMENT ACT
ENVIRONMENTAL PROTECTION ACT
FISHERIES ACT

BUILDING CODE ACT
EMPLOYMENT STANDARDS ACT
ENVIRONMENT ASSESSMENT ACT
ENVIRONMENT PROTECTION ACT
ENVIRONMENT MUNICIPAL ACT
TECHNICAL STANDARDS & SAFETY ACT
WASTE DIVERSION ACT
NUTRIENT MANAGEMENT ACT
FIRE PREVENTION & PROTECTION ACT
OCCUPATIONAL HEALTH & SAFETY ACT
ONTARIO WATER RESOURCES ACT
CONSOLIDATED HEARINGS ACT
AGGREGATED RESOURCES ACT
CONSERVATION AUTHORITIES ACT
ELECTRICITY ACT
ONTARIO PLUMBING CODE
HIGHWAY TRAFFIC ACT
PLANNING ACT

ONTARIO
CANADA

ENVIRO-POLICY

TIPPING MACHINES
CONTROLLING
CAPPING SYSTEM
seeded grasses
6" growing medium
24" protective cover
40 mil LLDPE
18" compacted clay
DEPOSITING
GASSES
COMPACTING
GRADING
SOLIDS
PILING
CAPPING
MATERIAL
MANAGEMENT

PUMPS
CELL BASE SUMPS
HOLDING TANKS
PLASTIC LINERS
EXTRACTING
RE-CIRCULATING
LIQUIDS
COLLECTING
CONTROLLING

TECHNOLOGY

AIRSPACE
IMPACT
MANAGEMENT
FOGGING SYSTEMS
STRATA CONFIGURATION
GEOLOGY
SITE
ON-SITE FEATURES
LOCATION
SITE ADJACENCIES
SITE ACCESS
ONE TIME
OPERATION
LANDFILL
SYSTEM CONFIGURATION & CONSTRUCTION
CAPPING
ROUTINE
WASTE MANAGEMENT
LEACHATE MANAGEMENT
METHANE HARVESTING
IMPACT CONTROL
POST CLOSURE

RECEIVING · SCALE HOUSE
TIPPING
COVERING
INSPECTION
WEIGHING
COLLECTION
ORGANIZED UNLOADING
GRADING
CIRCULATION
COMPACTING
DAILY SOIL COVER
ODOUR
DAILY APPROVED MAT
TRAFFIC
GROUNDWATER CONTAMINATION

LEACHATE MAINTENANCE
WATER QUALITY MONITORING
STORM WATER MANAGEMENT
SLOPE STABILITY MAINTENANCE
FINAL COVER MAINTENANCE
RESTRICTING ACCESS
LANDFILL GAS REMOVAL

24

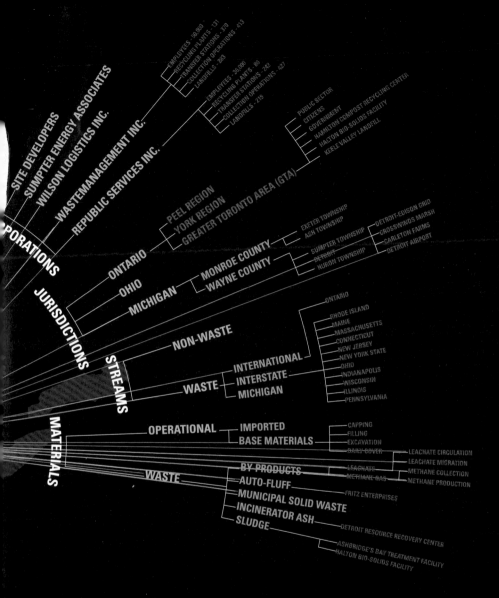

LAND RESERVATIONS

A call to extend the agency of landfills to organize open space networks

LAND RESERVATIONS: LANDFILL AS CONNECTOR

Wayne County, Michigan, United States. 42°05' N, 83°25'W

In Southeast Michigan, open spaces are defined as being composed of four primary types: wetlands, cultural parks, grasslands, and active agricultural land. While wetlands and cultural parks have a safeguarded status, grasslands and active agricultural fields are in a more vulnerable position, as the region's current development plan doesn't grant them any protection. With these land types' removal, the open space network experiences a significant reduction in its continuity.

At the moment of their conception, landfills are located at a point of equilibrium, where their distance from developed regions minimizes operational impacts while maintaining an economic proximity to sources of waste. When we examine the outward growth of urban centers such

as Detroit into the surrounding Wayne County, this rationale fails to hold. Ironically, four of the six active landfills within the county are now surrounded by development that emerged after the landfills were opened. Thus, the existence of a landfill does not preclude development around it.

Active agriculture once reserved open spaces, so why not now deploy another industrious, open space–preserving land use in order to regain some of the lost connectivity? Why not use the landfill as part of a land reservation system? Landfills inherently preserve open space since they cannot be built upon. Land Reservations explores the unutilized potential of landfill sites to structure, organize, and connect the open space network.

Absorbing Landfills in Sprawl
Detroit's growth, paired with landfill locations and opening dates: once-exurban sites become engulfed by development.

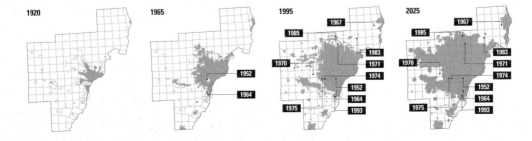

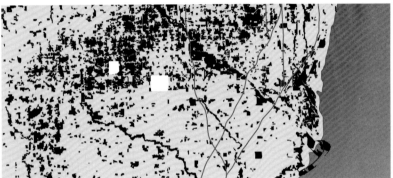

Landfill as Connector
The top two images show the existing open-space network of southern Wayne County (in black) and the potential fragmentation of this network should unprotected land uses be lost to development. In the image below, landfill sites are strategically deployed to reverse this process, stitching islands of open space into a continuous fabric.

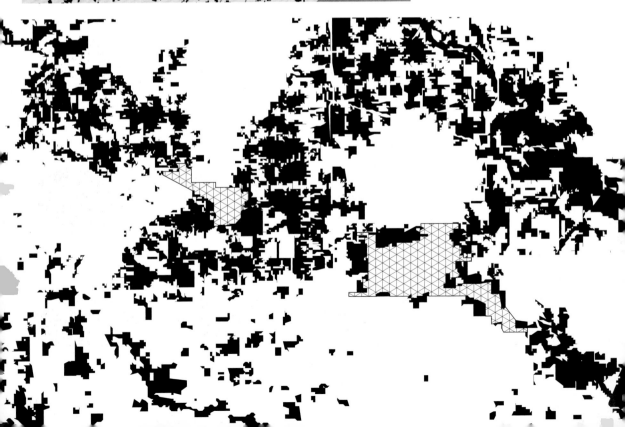

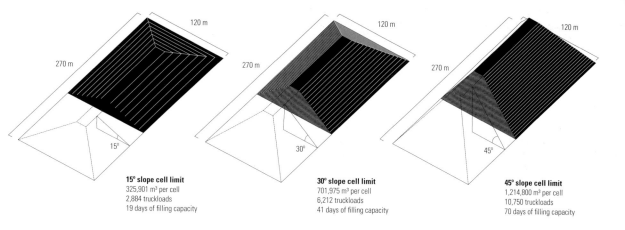

15° slope cell limit
325,901 m³ per cell
2,884 truckloads
19 days of filling capacity

30° slope cell limit
701,975 m³ per cell
6,212 truckloads
41 days of filling capacity

45° slope cell limit
1,214,800 m³ per cell
10,750 truckloads
70 days of filling capacity

Cell Morphology

The basic building block of a landfill is a cell—the active dumping site within the landfill bounds. The filling sequence is planned to optimize the capacity of the site as a whole, and is limited primarily by waste materials' angle of repose. When considerations are expanded to anticipate post-landfilling programs, a much wider variety of geometries becomes plausible.

FLATROCK, MI

RE-RIGGING

The Caspian Sea's oil rig field is retrofitted for post-oil occupation by wildlife, maverick entrepreneurs, and adventure seekers.

RE-RIGGING: OCCUPYING THE CASPIAN SEA

Caspian Sea, Caucasus Region 41°18' N, 50°57' E

The Caspian Sea is at the frontier of global offshore oil operations. Since the dissolution of the Soviet Union, the world's largest inland water body and the oil beneath it have been caught in the turmoil of shifting global powers. The site of the world's first offshore oil platform in 1947, extraction in the Caspian slowed in the 1960s, as the Soviet regime focused on newer, more easily exploitable fields. But in 1991, the sea was suddenly available—a largely untapped reservoir that attracted a collection of major and minor actors.

The United States, the European Union, regional powers, oil companies, international financial institutions, and nationalist movements anticipated the opportunities latent in the Caspian's seabed. Before these opportunities could be realized, however, the redivision of the sea among its new claimants required resolution. Three new littoral states—Turkmenistan, Azerbaijan, and Kazakhstan—inserted their claims into what had been a stable agreement between Russia and Iran. While dispute over the territory continues, it is certain that rigs will be installed, pipelines will flow, and the oil will be exploited.

Even as this occurs, it is increasingly clear that the petroleum economy and its associated operations have a limited life span. The Caspian Sea will remain beyond the moment when the last barrel of oil leaves its seabed. Is it possible to extend the momentum generated by the oil operations with a strategy that envisions the post-oil future of the sea? Can we plan for this moment as a new phase in the life of the sea, rather than passively anticipating a postindustrial wasteland?

500 km

Caspian Sea
371, 000 km²

Great Lakes
245, 580km²

Lake Victoria
68, 800km²

Lake Tanganyika
32,900km²

World's Largest Inland Water Body
The Caspian Sea does not fall neatly into the categories of maritime law, as it is inland and isolated from the world's oceans like a lake, but saline like a sea.

Nine Seas
The Caspian Sea is a complex of many interacting systems. Points of contact between agents, flows, and operations are hot spots for potential strategic intervention.

BATHYMETRY

SOVIET ERA: NATIONAL BOUNDARIES

POST SOVIET ERA: NATIONAL BOUNDARIES WITH CONTESTED REGION

OIL FIELDS: DEPOSITS, CONCESSION SYSTEMS, AND CONTRACT BLOCKS

OIL RIGS: EXISTING AND PROJECTED EXPANSION

BIRD TERRITORY: EXISTING AND PROJECTED EXPANSION

STURGEON TERRITORY: SPAWNING, FEEDING, AND WINTERING

TRANSPORTATION: RAIL, PORTS, PIPELINES, AND FERRY ROUTES

SITES AND PLAYERS: EXISTING AND PROJECTED EXPANSION

Offshore Oil-Extraction Sites

The position of rigs within the sea is registered against many factors. Oil fields, political boundaries, available contract blocks, jurisdictional concession systems, pipeline tanker routes, and ports all influence their location.

Water Birds

The western coast of the Caspian Sea is a major flyway, supporting the migration of more than twenty million water birds each year. Typically these birds stay close to the shore, within fifteen kilometers of a landing. As development has destroyed their habitat along the coast, many birds have claimed abandoned oil rigs as resting points along their routes.

Bathymetry

Surface area: 3/1,000 km²
Volume: 78,200 km³

The Northern Caspian is a shallow shelf; it accounts for less than 1 percent of the sea's total water volume, with average depths of 5-6 meters. The sea drops off toward its middle where the average depth increases to 190 meters. The deepest zones are found in the Southern Caspian, where depths reach more than 1000 meters.

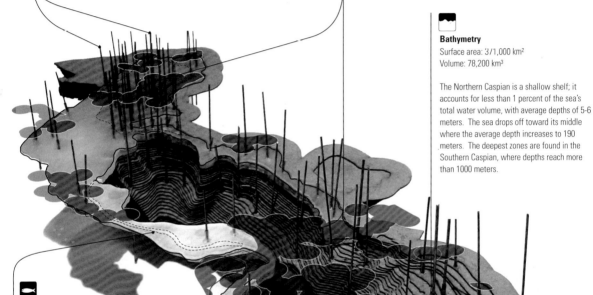

Caspian Sturgeon

The sea is home to a variety of fish species, including sturgeon, from which more than 90 percent of the world's caviar is harvested. As inland spawning grounds and coastal habitats are degraded by development and poaching, the offshore oil installations have become an important alternative sanctuary. Acting as artificial reefs, the structures provide surfaces that support the growth of plant life, which in turn supplies food for the fish.

The life of a sturgeon is divided into three phases. Spawning takes place in the spring in the freshwater rivers feeding the sea. The fish then spend most of the year feeding in the shallower northern regions. In the winter the sturgeon migrate south along the sea's western coast to warmer waters.

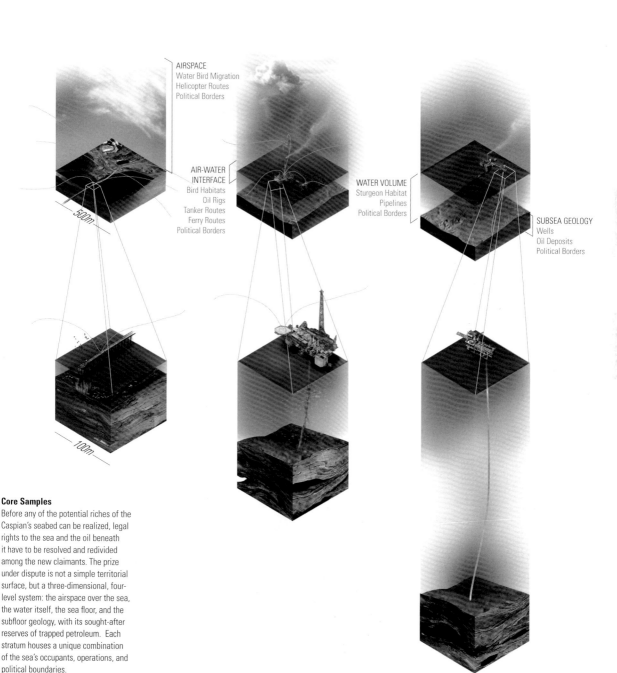

AIRSPACE
Water Bird Migration
Helicopter Routes
Political Borders

AIR-WATER
INTERFACE
Bird Habitats
Oil Rigs
Tanker Routes
Ferry Routes
Political Borders

WATER VOLUME
Sturgeon Habitat
Pipelines
Political Borders

SUBSEA GEOLOGY
Wells
Oil Deposits
Political Borders

500m

100m

Core Samples

Before any of the potential riches of the Caspian's seabed can be realized, legal rights to the sea and the oil beneath it have to be resolved and redivided among the new claimants. The prize under dispute is not a simple territorial surface, but a three-dimensional, four-level system: the airspace over the sea, the water itself, the sea floor, and the subfloor geology, with its sought-after reserves of trapped petroleum. Each stratum houses a unique combination of the sea's occupants, operations, and political boundaries.

Reconnecting

Rig-to-rig connections are rare in the current operational model, which privileges port-to-rig linkages. As the number of rigs in the sea increases, there is potential to lessen the intensity at the land-based hub and create direct connections between rigs.

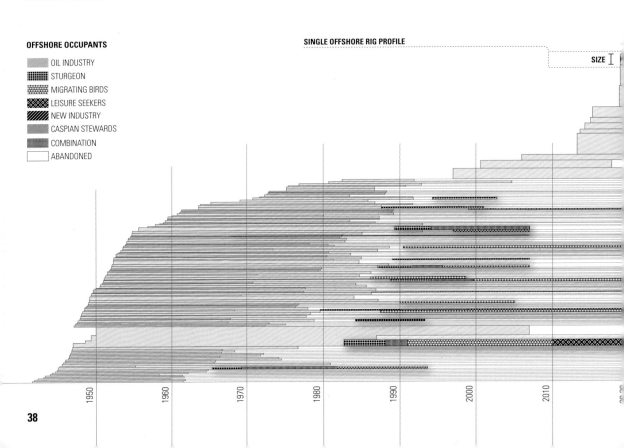

2010

2035

Projected Reoccupations

The diagram below shows projected activity in the Caspian Sea up to 2100. As oil extraction declines, opportunities for alternative economies and ecosystems emerge. A clue to this reoccupation can be found in the changing migratory patterns of Caspian water birds, who have adapted their routes to take advantage of the surfaces of abandoned platforms. A host of opportunistic new occupants might find niches as more such sites become available.

OFFSHORE OCCUPANTS

- OIL INDUSTRY
- STURGEON
- MIGRATING BIRDS
- LEISURE SEEKERS
- NEW INDUSTRY
- CASPIAN STEWARDS
- COMBINATION
- ABANDONED

SINGLE OFFSHORE RIG PROFILE

SIZE

1950   1960   1970   1980   1990   2000   2010

PEAK PRESENCE OF OIL OPERATIONS

L-RELATED OPERATIONAL LIFESPAN   ABANDONED CONDITION   PROPOSED REACTIVATION

2030   2040   2050   2060   2070   2080   2090   2100

Reoccupying

Sparsely dotted over the vast sea, the constructed surfaces of the rigs are at a premium. Sectional site studies offer a strategy for maximizing these surfaces vertically, offsetting the strata of the rigs to increase the occupiable area. As wildlife and human populations shift and diversify, it is expected that the scarce but valuable surfaces will attract new occupants. This offline oil-extraction platform is transformed into an accommodation and gateway unit for leisure and adventure seekers.

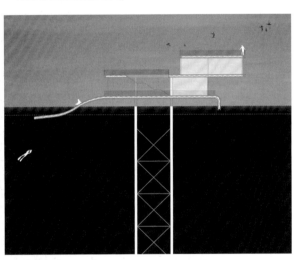

Reexploiting

The Caspian Sea currently represents the frontier of oil exploration and exploitation. It is projected that oil extraction will peak between 2020 and 2030. When the oil companies begin to wind down their operations, the key to the proposed renewal of the sea will be the re-exploitation of the relics they leave behind. Here, a small offline oil platform, abandoned in the 1960s, has been transformed into a node along a network of bird-watching areas and dive sites.

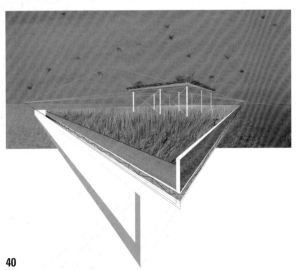

Reactivating

The relationship between the occupiable surface offered by the abandoned rigs and the territories of the sea's occupants becomes more evident as years pass. The development that followed the building of the rigs rendered parts of the shoreline inhospitable to water birds. The less obvious result of the human incursion is that the now-deserted structures have begun to offer birds new stop-over points along flyways and provide fish new reef-like habitats—expanding their territories' bounds.

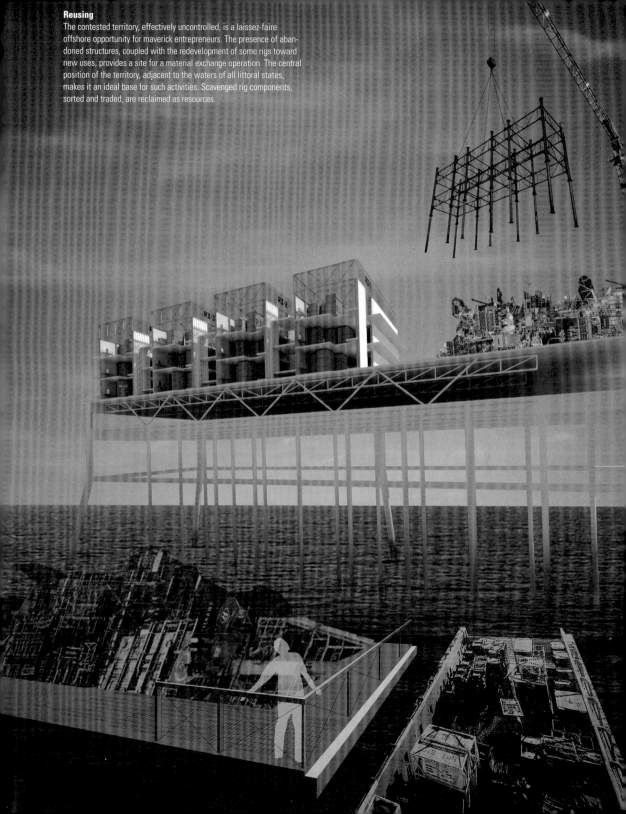

Reusing
The contested territory, effectively uncontrolled, is a laissez-faire offshore opportunity for maverick entrepreneurs. The presence of abandoned structures, coupled with the redevelopment of some rigs toward new uses, provides a site for a material exchange operation. The central position of the territory, adjacent to the waters of all littoral states, makes it an ideal base for such activities. Scavenged rig components, sorted and traded, are reclaimed as resources.

THE ARCHITECTURAL RECONSTRUCTION OF GEOGRAPHY

David Gissen

Terms such as "research," "organization," "landscape," and "infrastructure" define many of the activities of contemporary architects seeking to find a new framework for architectural processes and design. But we might more adequately argue that a geographical character best describes the mental and material structure of this architecture. This involves not only a turn toward specific geographical concepts and theories, but toward material and representational transformations as well. We can see this in various contemporary works that advance the territory of maps over plans, the flow of matter over subjects, and the concept of environment over that of space-time. It's as if architects have simultaneously leaped over the city as the perceptual scale within which architecture might operate and rejected the Anglo-American concept of region as architecture's ultimate physical and analogical correlate. Today, a select number of architects attempt to rebuild geography with architecture—a project in which buildings bring their own territorial concerns into focus.

The geographical project of architecture is symptomatic of a shake-up concerning the very realms that architectural design negotiates. Design, as it was conceptualized in both the interwar and postwar periods of the twentieth century, was a practice positioned at the intersection of labor, governance, and industry. Space-time, as it emerged within the rise of industrializing states, was the very thing shaped by design. In many ways, design contained a utopian notion—a force that could negotiate the space-time tissues of experience and an idea that could bring its agents (proletariat, state, and bourgeoisie) into unity. It's clear to virtually all who are surveying the contemporary situation that the relations between these agents are falling apart. Labor neither constitutes an autonomous, isolated force (i.e., "the masses") nor a sole class—it has become something more amorphous. Sadly, states are suspect on the right and left, and industry has so atomized itself that it cannot be located with any precision. Governance, production, and management are simultaneously everywhere and nowhere, or, to put it another way, they occupy spaces outside the perceptual space-time of an individual subject. Those who adhere to design in its early-twentieth-century incarnation have the fascinating role of devotees to a form of modern antiquity, even as they search for the new. At its most extreme, we have contemporary architects who find heroism within the movements of space itself and the computerized, multi-axial routers that form it. This extends architects' emotional and intellectual investment in the forms of production driven by modernity, but with zero transformative potential on the constituent actors. More convincing are those architects who attempt to reduce the amorphous quality of contemporary experience into a more intelligible urban and political whole. But such work often operates at the scales of the

Mem.de l'Acad. des Sciences 1741. page 336.
Pl. 10.

Flood of the Seine, Philippe Buache, 1740: The early tensions between architectural and geographical projects for the city can be seen in his map of the Paris flood of 1740. Buache was trained as an architect, but ultimately turned to geography to articulate his particular intellectual interests.

ndustrial city—room, courtyard, region— without the necessary constituent actors.

As for the geographic experiment within contemporary architecture, its architects do not simply reject the ideology of design. Rather, at its most incisive, geography takes on more of a meta role—as part of a technique that articulates and distributes the potential of architectural authorship within an intellectual territory. For example, maps illustrate givens for many contemporary architects (in the weak literalness of so-called reality mapping exercises), but much more powerful are maps that illustrate the search for an arena for the architect. In this instance, maps not only show

facts (the locations of towns, rivers, and other socio-natural features), they also provide commentary on where architectural ideas will appear and when. Within a large area, they articulate where the architect's thoughts will and will not be, where his or her effects will be felt and where not. These maps represent the crisis of authorship that defines the contemporary field, while still demonstrating the capacity of human beings to shape large arenas. And though maps figure prominently in geographical work, geographically oriented architects do not necessarily design buildings at the literal scale of the map; their work can be as small as a street lamp. Nevertheless, whether they author a massive bridge proposal

Paris Expo Plan, OMA, 1985: This important and early carto-organizational project, which extends the ideas of nineteenth-century urbanist Ildefons Cerda and late-modern experimentalists Archizoom, continues to influence geo-architectural works. The design of a precinct's plan is reduced to a geographical system of longitude and latitude. The squares denote areas of potential architectural authorship.

or the tiniest piece of street furniture, their aim is similar: to bring designed objects into cartographic narratives. Such work searches for a theory of architecture relative to geography, similar to architects' search for a theory of architecture relative to the city. Similarly, drawn sections articulate the flows of social and natural matter relative to the project, versus the psychological sense of space within a building. Such sections emphasize the articulation of material through a territory or on a person, rather than the specific experience of individuals. Significantly, the entire connective tissue of the geographical within architecture is the redesign of "environment." Geographically oriented work is not simply anti-spatial; environment is spatial and temporal, but relations between space and time are beholden to the constituent features of the environment. In turn, these redesigned environments create new forms and ideas about the geographical.

The above descriptions should not be taken as blanket endorsements of these particular practices. The new geographical architecture contains many frustrating tendencies. If architects choose to work at the limit of geography versus the limit of the city, then the best of these new geo-architects might begin a more self-reflective phase—interrogating the aesthetic and historical implications of maps, vectors, and environments. Unlike plans, sections, and spaces, geographical forms of representation tend to take on the mask of natural reality versus representational forms. And in some hands, geography can be turned into a frightening tool to make architectural interventions appear as works of nature, rather than acting as another system for architects to use to tinker with reality. Design and design pedagogy contain forceful and articulate relationships to history, within notions of "parti," "precedent," and "referent." These historically driven terms would sound absurd within most of the geographically oriented architecture of today. Geographical concepts are notoriously ahistorical, and geographers often use this to challenge the primacy of

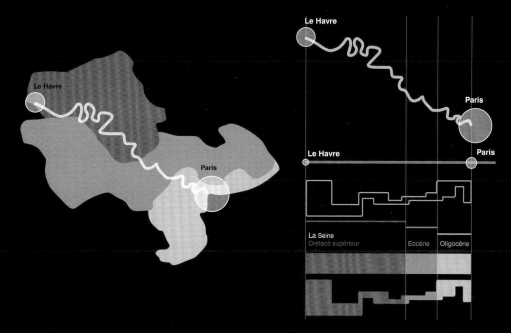

Air Map of Paris, Philippe Rahm, 2007: Rahm's project proposes condensing the historic path of air movement from Le Havre to Paris into a single mechanical system for a Parisian office building. Here geo-architecture engages cartography, matter, and environment, but ultimately is disentangled from the literal space of the map and takes on a representational and historical dimension.

history within a society's established forms of self-understanding. But the ahistoricity of geography generally, and geographical imagery within architecture more specifically, needs to be questioned and interrogated. When architects bring aesthetics and history into geographical concepts, they transform an environment into something more unfamiliar and monumental. The flows of matter will slow down, and the environment will begin to appear as an object, even as we find ourselves immersed within it. Through such work, architecture will begin to show how environments are historical constructions versus natural ones. In turn, this work might reveal the geographical chain that moves through all of architecture and the architecture of our future geography.

David Gissen, Ph.D., is Associate Professor of Architecture and Visual Arts at The California College of the Arts.

ALERT (5)

GRISE FJORD (160)

ARCTIC BAY (640)
NANISIVIK

RESOLUTE (230)

ARCTIC OCEAN

02

CAMBRIDGE BAY (1160)

SACHS HARBOUR (122)

ULUKHAKTOK (398)

PAULATUK (294)

KUGLUKTUK (1198)

TUKTOYAKTUK (870)

01

AKLAVIK (594)
INUVIK (3484)

FORT MCPHERSON (761)
TSIIGEHTCHIC (175)

COLVILLE LAKE (126)

GREAT BEAR LAKE

FORT GOOD HOPE (557)

NORMAN WELLS (761)

WEKWEETI (137)

UNITED STATES
CANADA

TULITA (505)
DELINE (529)

GAMETI (238)

YELLOWKNIFE (19569)
WHATI (460)
BEHCHOKO (1894)
DETTAH (241)

WRIGLEY (122)

GREAT SLAVE

ARCTIC CIRCLE
66°

FORT SIMPSON (1216)
JEAN MARIE RIVER (61)

FORT PROVIDENCE (727)
KAKISA (52)

HAY RIVER (3648)
ENTERPRISE (87)

FORT RESOL

ATLANTIC OCEAN

CLYDE RIVER (790)

QIKIQTARJUAQ (495)

PANGNIRTUNG (1240)

IQALUIT (3595)

03

KIMMIRUT (385)

IGLOOLIK (1440)

HALL BEACH (624)

QUAQTAQ (315)

KANGIQSUJUAQ (605)

KANGIRSUK (465)

KANGIQSUALUJJUAQ (735)

CAPE DORSET (1197)

KANGIQSUJUAQ (605)

SALLUIT (1241)

AUPALUK (174)

KUUJJUAQ (2132)

KUGAARUK (640)

TASIUJAQ (268)

IVUJIVIK (349)

REPULSE BAY (710)

CORAL HARBOUR (735)

AKULIVIK (507)

PUVIRNITUQ (4527)

INUKJUAK (1597)

CHESTERFIELD INLET (290)

HUDSON BAY

BAKER LAKE (1728)

RANKIN INLET (1925)

WHALE COVE (335)

ARVIAT (2060)

NEXT NORTH

A series of proposals centered on the
ecological and social empowerment
of Canada's unique Far North and its
attendant networks

CHURCHILL (923)

M'SELL PORTAGE (150)
TIRANIT CITY (85)
FOND DU LAC (801)

LAKE ATHABASCA

NEXT NORTH: CANADA'S HIGH ARCTIC
North of 60°N

The myth of Canada is often preceded by the unique geography of the Canadian North—a vast, sparsely populated, fragile, and sublime territory. Yet with one of the most dramatically changing climates on Earth and an estimated quarter of the planet's undiscovered energy resources, this Arctic region has emerged as a site of significant economic and developmental speculation. It is a frontier again. The balance in which ecologies and people coexist in this region, and the complexity of the interaction between national politics and local cultures, cannot be overstated. The region's unique combination of climate, culture, and geography produces complicated infrastructures, settlements, and sociopolitical negotiations. The melting of polar ice has given rise to territorial land claims, threatened ecosystems, uncovered new resources, and an intensified interest in the northern frontier.

Nations with territorial adjacencies to the Arctic Ocean are rushing to lay claim to its resource-rich waters and to define their sovereign rights. Northern Canadian settlements have traditionally expanded under the pressure of previous diamond and gold rushes, and along with the emerging oil and gas rushes, the federal government anticipates the creation of deep-sea ports and military bases.

However, with this urgency to expand, there is little vision of development beyond economic expediency and efficiency.

Throughout the twentieth century, the Canadian North had a sordid and unfortunate history of colonial enterprises, political maneuverings, and non-integrated development proposals that perpetuated sovereign control and economic development. Northern developments are intimately tied to the construction of infrastructure, though these projects are rarely conceived with a long-term, holistic vision. How might future infrastructures participate in cultivating and perpetuating ecosystems and local cultures, rather than threatening them? How might Arctic settlements respond more directly to the exigencies of this transforming climate and geography, and its ever-increasing pressures from the South? What is next for the North?

As the effects of global warming take their full impact, polar regions could see the greatest change in human migration patterns. In Canada, more than 100,000 people are living north of 60° latitude for the first time in history, and more than 18,500 people are living above the Arctic Circle in 24

From left to right: Icebreaker opening a passage; Peary Caribou foraging for food; Clearing snow from an ice road; *Saxifraga oppositifolia*—caribou food; Hamlet of Resolute; Convoy along an ice road

settlements. Furthermore, populations in the North are remarkably young. For example, in the town of Iqaluit, Nunavut, 60 percent of the population is under twenty-five years old, ensuring rapid population growth for the next several decades.

While territorial claims of this "New Cold War" are being negotiated, they offer a unique chance to question how development should occur. Infrastructure in the Canadian North has often been based on systems used in the south of the country, which are permanent and independent structures that are difficult to upgrade or alter. A wider understanding of an environment that unpredictably oscillates between freeze and thaw, dark and light, accessible and inaccessible, tradition and technology would allow for infrastructural opportunities that maintain soft, multivalent, and malleable characteristics. A characteristic of ecosystems—as complex systems that are able to negotiate hierarchies and scales—provides a dynamic precedent for infrastructure in the Arctic. How might infrastructure be adaptable, responsive, and temporal? Soft infrastructure offers the possibility of fusing existing systems with emergent ones to catalyze a network of ecologies and economies for a new public realm in the Arctic.

Recognizing that the challenges for Arctic inhabitation extend beyond merely designing better homes or new technologies, Next North looks at the roles and challenges of the public realm, civic space, landscape, and infrastructure. While infrastructure in the Canadian North has often consisted of single-use, large-scale regional networks or small-scale products, the following projects remain more interested in geographic scalability, environmental adaptability, and multiuse programmability. Next North charts this 3.5-million-square-kilometer context through six themes: transport, ecologies, settlements, research, culture, and resources. Potential crossovers are sought to leverage and test dormant or overlooked opportunities. The three representative projects selected here address issues of transportation, ecologies, and education, and utilize soft systems that respond to climatic variation, programmatic needs, and cultural diversity.

ICE ROAD TRUCK STOPS (01)

The Contwoyto Winter Road, first constructed in 1982 to give access to diamond and gold mining sites north of Yellowknife, the Northwest Territories, is almost 355 miles long, with about 87 percent of its surface built on frozen lakes. Open for trucking only sixty-seven days on average during the winter, the ice road reverts to water for the rest of the year, leaving the truck stops isolated and abandoned.

The project consists of a series of intersecting meshes that address road reinforcement, energy capture, and aquatic ecologies. The mesh is installed at critical shorelines just below the water's surface, serving to reinforce ice roads during the winter and invigorate lake ecologies during warmer seasons. As trucks travel over the ice road, a hydrodynamic wave forms below the ice, which the mesh captures and converts to energy through a proposed buoy network. These same buoys are also outfitted with flooding nozzles at the water surface and artificial reefs along the cable and at the lakebed. As the mesh reaches land, it thickens to form the primary shells of a truck stop complex (winter) and fishing camp (summer).

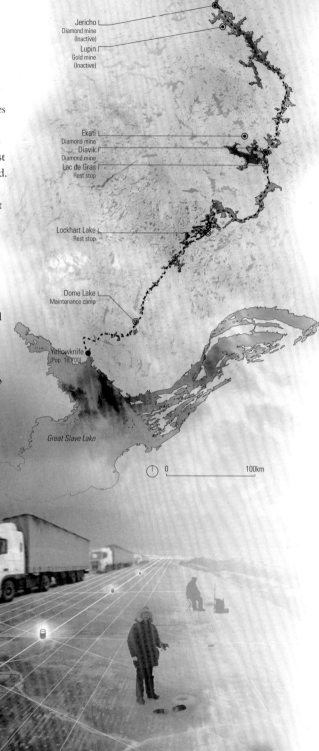

Jericho
Diamond mine
(Inactive)

Lupin
Gold mine
(Inactive)

Ekati
Diamond mine

Diavik
Diamond mine

Lac de Gras
Rest stop

Lockhart Lake
Rest stop

Dome Lake
Maintenance camp

Yellowknife
(Pop. 18,700)

Great Slave Lake

0   100km

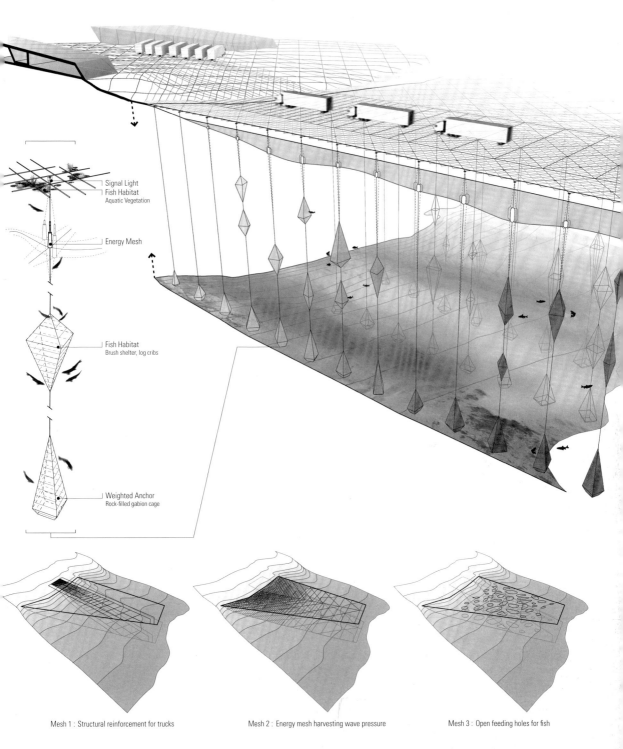

Signal Light
Fish Habitat
Aquatic Vegetation

Energy Mesh

Fish Habitat
Brush shelter, log cribs

Weighted Anchor
Rock-filled gabion cage

Mesh 1 : Structural reinforcement for trucks

Mesh 2 : Energy mesh harvesting wave pressure

Mesh 3 : Open feeding holes for fish

CARIBOU PIVOT STATIONS (02)

This project capitalizes on the intersection between the anticipated eighty-five million dollars allocated to the Arctic Research Infrastructure Fund across Canada's Nunavut and the Northwest Territories and the region's threatened caribou, an integral species in the Arctic food web. The caribou population has declined considerably in recent decades: for example, there were forty thousand Peary Caribou in 1961, but only seven hundred in 2009. Unexpected temperature fluctuations have increased ice formation, making it difficult for migrating caribou to forage for Arctic ground cover. To address this, we propose new research station typologies, in which the station creates a microclimate or oasis of deflected and cleared snow and ice—a fresh foraging field. The building mass is inflected toward prevailing winds, while supplementary "snow screens" and ice-clearing pivot gantries manage snowfall for snow deflection, insulation, collection, or concealment.

Peary Carib
1974 :   4,5
1980 :   5,0
1995 :   1
2010 : unkno

SUMMER
Northern Ran

SPRING
Calving Grou
(Somerset

(Prince of Wales

FALL
Rutting Perio

McClintock
Channel

WINTER
Southern Ran

Resolute
(2,30)

Taloyoak ●
(Pop. 745)

● Cambridge Bay
(Pop. 1,477)

Gjoa Haven ●
(Pop. 990)

● Kugaar
(Pop. 64(

Type 1

1A

Type 2

2A

2B

Type 3

3A

3B

New Research Station Types
Architecture symbiotic with environment and ecology
rather than mitigating it

0   100km

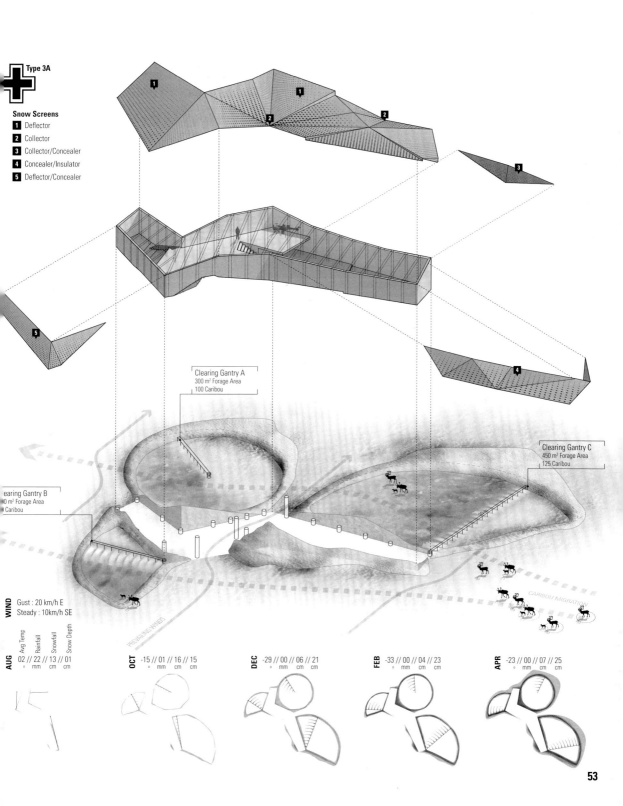

Type 3A

Snow Screens

1 Deflector
2 Collector
3 Collector/Concealer
4 Concealer/Insulator
5 Deflector/Concealer

Clearing Gantry A
300 m² Forage Area
100 Caribou

Clearing Gantry C
450 m² Forage Area
125 Caribou

Clearing Gantry B
00 m² Forage Area
Caribou

CARIBOU MIGRATION

WIND
Gust : 20 km/h E
Steady : 10km/h SE

PREVAILING WINDS

Avg Temp
Rainfall
Snowfall
Snow Depth

AUG 02 // 22 // 13 // 01
° mm cm cm

OCT -15 // 01 // 16 // 15
° mm cm cm

DEC -29 // 00 // 06 // 21
° mm cm cm

FEB -33 // 00 // 04 // 23
° mm cm cm

APR -23 // 00 // 07 // 25
° mm cm cm

LIQUID COMMONS (03)

Access to educational infrastructure is extremely challenging in remote areas such as Nunavut, Canada. Recent studies have found that more than half of Nunavut's working-age population and 80 percent of its youth (ages sixteen to twenty-five) struggle with literacy, an issue that Nunavut's premier suggests is at the root of poor housing conditions, high suicide rates, domestic violence, poverty, and lack of job skills. Liquid Commons provides a new, malleable educational infrastructure composed of a series of boats that travel between the harbors of eleven adjacent settlements, catering to more than seventy-five hundred "unserved" citizens. By disaggregating and transporting educational services, a larger selection of amenities is afforded to these locations. During the fall season, before the Hudson Strait freezes, the boats gather at flexible nodes along the icebreaker shipping route to create a central hub as well as a bridge across the icebreaker's fissure to allow connection between these settlements. By utilizing water as a distributor during the summer and as a shared connective platform in the winter, Liquid Commons becomes both a unifying network and a node.

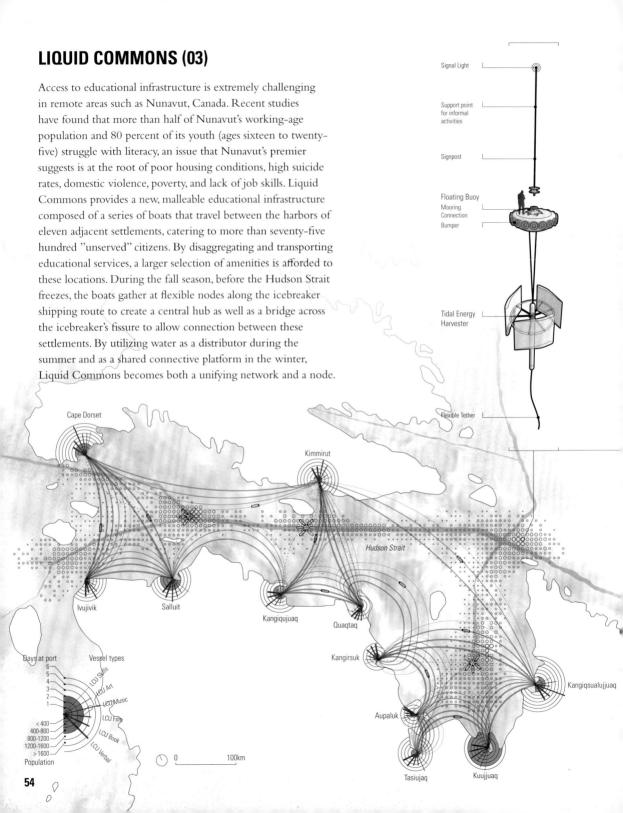

Signal Light

Support point for informal activities

Signpost

Floating Buoy
Mooring Connection
Bumper

Tidal Energy Harvester

Flexible Tether

Cape Dorset

Kimmirut

Hudson Strait

Ivujivik

Salluit

Kangiqujuaq

Quaqtaq

Kangirsuk

Kangiqsualujjuaq

Aupaluk

Days at port
6
5
4
3
2
1

Vessel types
LCU Skills
LCU Art
LCU Music
LCU Film
LCU Book
LCU Verbal

< 400
400–800
800–1200
1200–1600
> 1600
Population

0   100km

Tasiujaq   Kuujjuaq

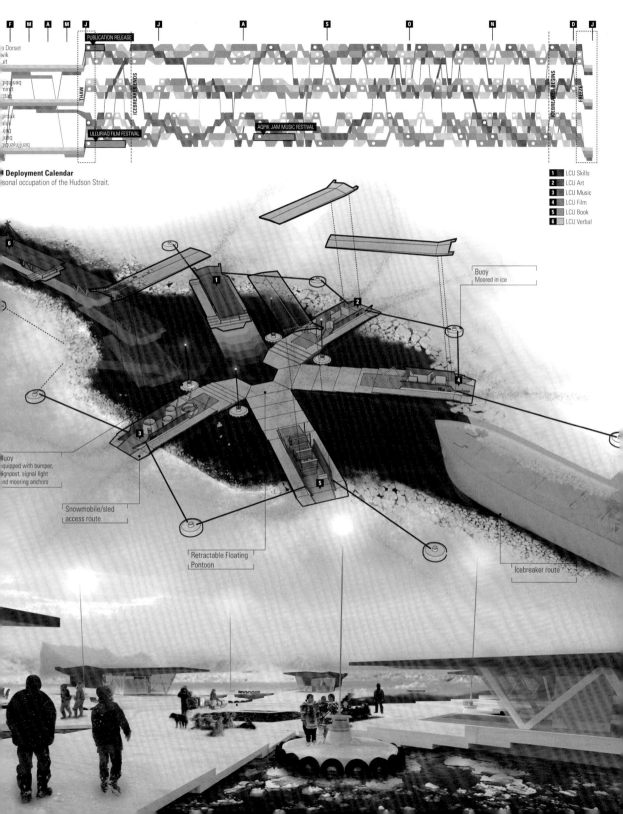

Deployment Calendar
Seasonal occupation of the Hudson Strait.

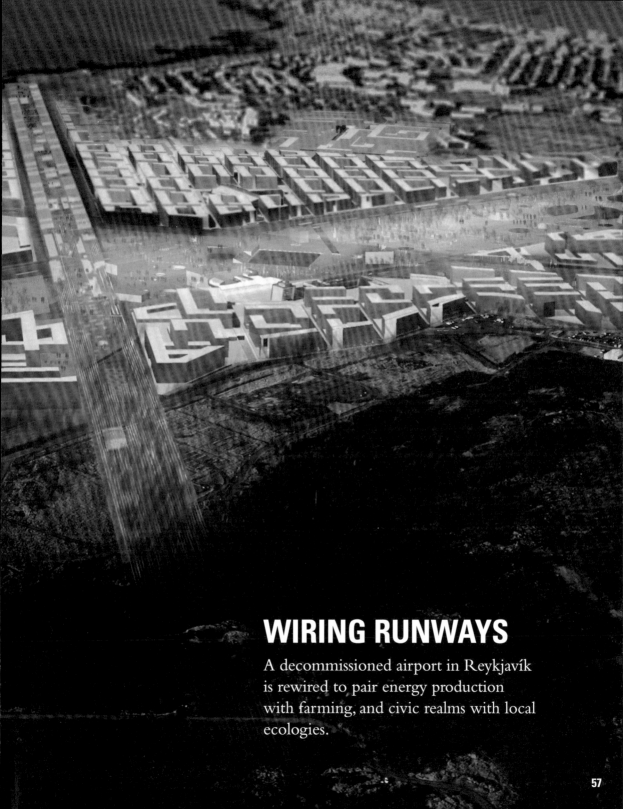

WIRING RUNWAYS

A decommissioned airport in Reykjavík
is rewired to pair energy production
with farming, and civic realms with local
ecologies.

WIRING RUNWAYS: FRAMING AND FARMING THE VOID

Reykjavík, Iceland 64°7' N, 21°56' W

The decommissioning of the Vatnsmýri Airport due to increasing land value offers the potential to create a new global node for Reykjavík while reengaging the infrastructure of the airport. Iceland is known for its rich history, its culture, and more recently, for its abundant geothermal energy. This energy is a result of Iceland's origins and geographic location—straddling the Mid-Atlantic ridge, the country consists of a dynamic landscape of several geologically active volcanoes.

Wiring Runways reinterprets the figural quality of the airport runways as three "no-build" public infrastructural axes, or Greenways, that are framed by four distinct urban zones. Each Greenway takes on a programmatic grouping: production, recreation, or civic and ecological. The Production Greenway reconfigures a bar code of activities—including aquaculture, greenhouses, allotment gardens, markets, and tree farms—into a symbiotic system. The Civic and Ecological Greenway is composed of a series of micro-ecologies that are paired and dotted with civic institutions. Organized as a corridor of outdoor rooms that are marked with figures of play, the Recreation Greenway encourages a rich mixing of diverse demographics. Within the development, four new block types privilege varying degrees of porosity, producing a gradient of public space in the development.

Running below and linking the Greenways is a global data server farm that capitalizes on Iceland's vast geothermal energy and remote location for its large cooling and security demands. The server farm continues the legacy of the Vatnsmýri area, linking Reykjavík to the world just as the airport once did.

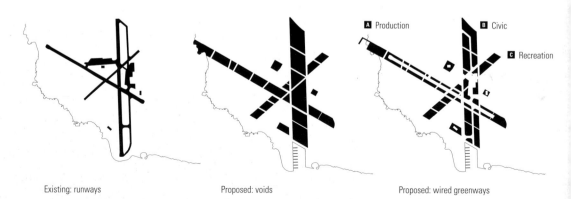

A Production B Civic C Recreation

Existing: runways   Proposed: voids   Proposed: wired greenways

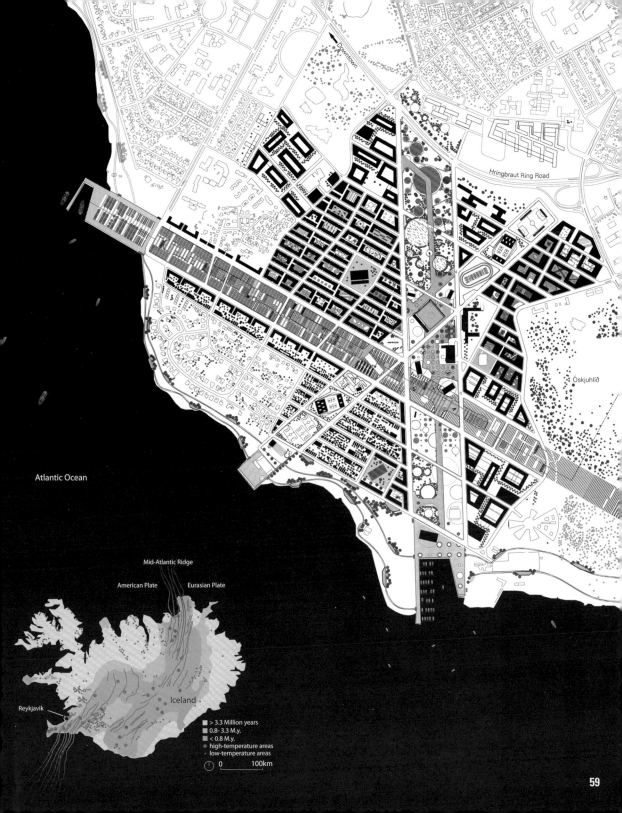

Downtown

Hringbraut Ring Road

Öskjuhlið

Atlantic Ocean

Mid-Atlantic Ridge

American Plate   Eurasian Plate

Iceland

Reykjavik

■ > 3.3 Million years
■ 0.8- 3.3 M.y.
■ < 0.8 M.y.
● high-temperature areas
· low-temperature areas

⊙ 0   100km

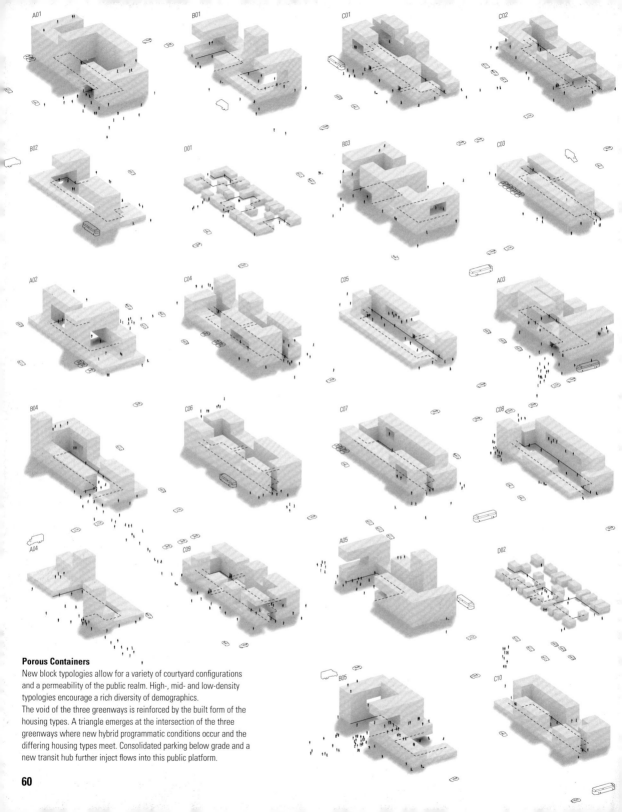

Porous Containers

New block typologies allow for a variety of courtyard configurations and a permeability of the public realm. High-, mid- and low-density typologies encourage a rich diversity of demographics.

The void of the three greenways is reinforced by the built form of the housing types. A triangle emerges at the intersection of the three greenways where new hybrid programmatic conditions occur and the differing housing types meet. Consolidated parking below grade and a new transit hub further inject flows into this public platform.

1. wetlands, 2. school, 3. cinema, 4. community center,
5. athletic center, 6. ice rink, 7. hotel, 8. bike share,
9. transit hub, 10. cinema, 11. greenhouses, 12. market,
13. aviation museum , 14. playground, 15. school,
16. botanic center, 17. cultural center

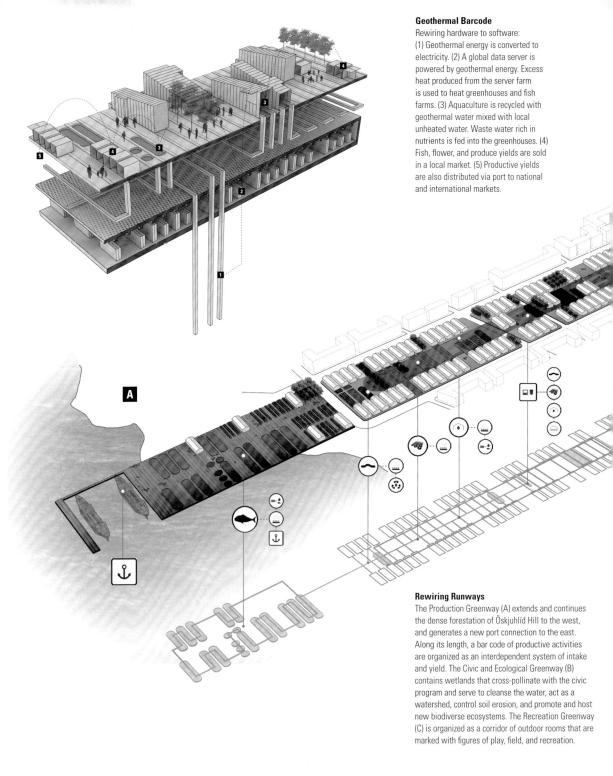

Geothermal Barcode

Rewiring hardware to software:
(1) Geothermal energy is converted to electricity. (2) A global data server is powered by geothermal energy. Excess heat produced from the server farm is used to heat greenhouses and fish farms. (3) Aquaculture is recycled with geothermal water mixed with local unheated water. Waste water rich in nutrients is fed into the greenhouses. (4) Fish, flower, and produce yields are sold in a local market. (5) Productive yields are also distributed via port to national and international markets.

Rewiring Runways

The Production Greenway (A) extends and continues the dense forestation of Öskjuhlíd Hill to the west, and generates a new port connection to the east. Along its length, a bar code of productive activities are organized as an interdependent system of intake and yield. The Civic and Ecological Greenway (B) contains wetlands that cross-pollinate with the civic program and serve to cleanse the water, act as a watershed, control soil erosion, and promote and host new biodiverse ecosystems. The Recreation Greenway (C) is organized as a corridor of outdoor rooms that are marked with figures of play, field, and recreation.

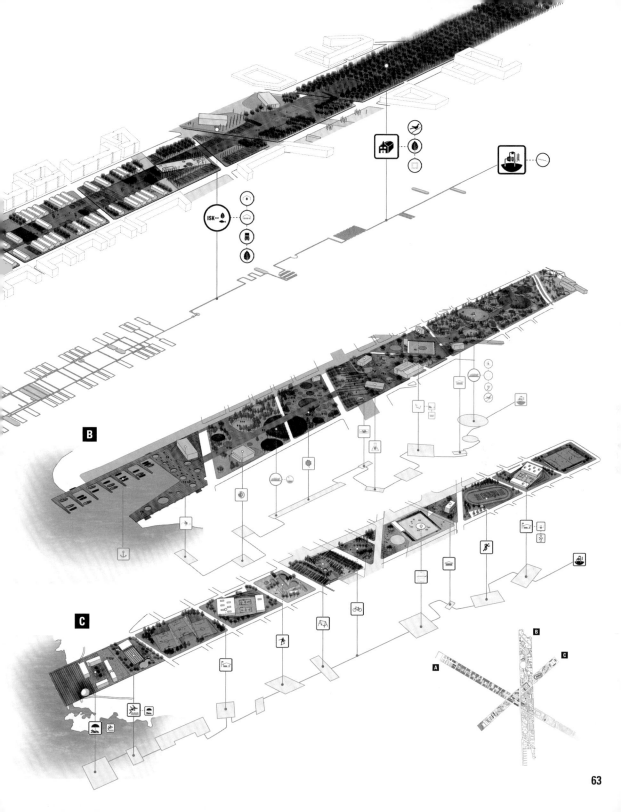

Geothermal Energy

Water Management

Trees

Harvesting Networks
Networks of energy, water management, and tree farms intersect with new public programs at the void of the runways, injecting production into the public sphere.

ICELINK

A former land bridge at the Bering Strait
provides an opportunity to bundle high-
speed rail, ice harvesting, and environment
monitoring.

ICELINK: OCCUPYING THE TEMPORAL SEAM

Bering Strait, Russia/United States 65°30' N, 169°00' W

It would be difficult to find a site more geographically charged than the Bering Strait. A region rich in scientific speculation, exploration, resources, ecology, and myth, the remote position of the strait has relegated it to the role of a global seam, a spatial and temporal rift. IceLink consists of two primary infrastructural elements: an ecological park and a tunnel-bridge link. The tunnel surfaces to reveal a bridge as it approaches the international date line to establish a port and public walkway. The park intensifies the existing phenomenon of ice-floe collection that happens in the shallow space between the Diomede Islands.

The Bering Strait is part of a rich cycle of north-south exchange that is heavily informed by seasonal changes. As the summer months thaw the ice shelf, causing it to migrate northwards, freshwater is released into the sea. The natural production of ice allows for the storage of precious freshwater, which is increasingly threatened. The current water crisis has left more than 884 million people without access to safe drinking water. IceLink harvests water for two purposes: to conserve freshwater before it thaws into the seas and to increase freshwater production in order to infuse more into the seas and promote phytoplankton production, forming a robust foundation to the oceans' food chain.

Straddling the international date line and the United States/Russia border, IceLink is an ideal zone of diplomatic, cultural, and economic exchange. New programs that promote exchange envelop the bridge and spatialize the symbolic significance of this link. Infrastructural, resource-based, and ecological flows in and around the Bering Strait create a central node that connects its surroundings with global impact.

Ice Trap and Release
The Bering Strait land bridge repeats more ephemerally today through ice formation and accumulation.

Ice Park
Sea ice is trapped between the Diomedes prior to drifting northward. The new ice park seeks to enhance and intensify this phenomenon by cultivating, collecting, and distributing ice floes.

Jan   Feb   Mar   Apr   May   Jun   Jul   Aug   Sep   Oct   Nov   Dec

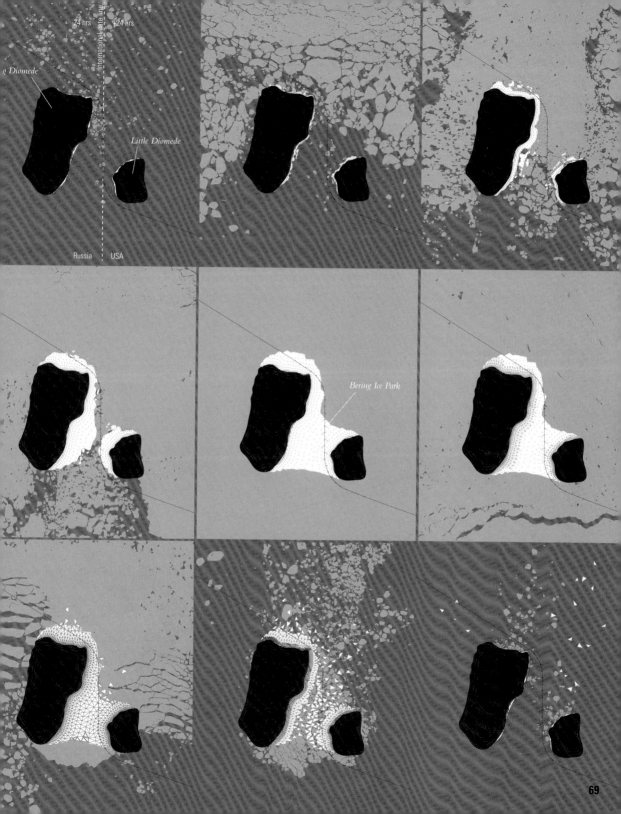

g Diomede

International date line

24 hrs | +24 hrs

Little Diomede

Russia | USA

Bering Ice Park

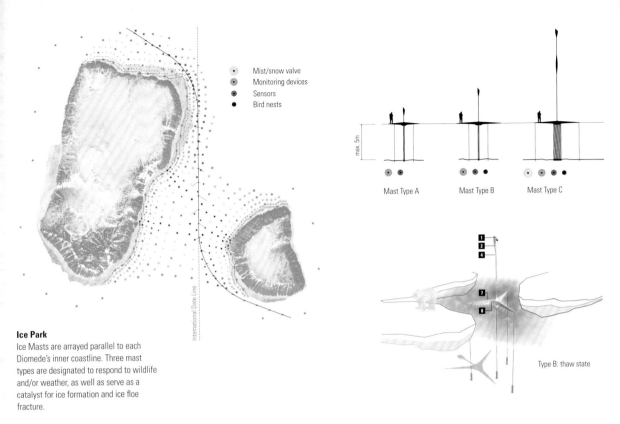

Mist/snow valve
Monitoring devices
Sensors
Bird nests

Mast Type A   Mast Type B   Mast Type C

max. 5m

International Date Line

Ice Park

Ice Masts are arrayed parallel to each Diomede's inner coastline. Three mast types are designated to respond to wildlife and/or weather, as well as serve as a catalyst for ice formation and ice floe fracture.

Type B: thaw state

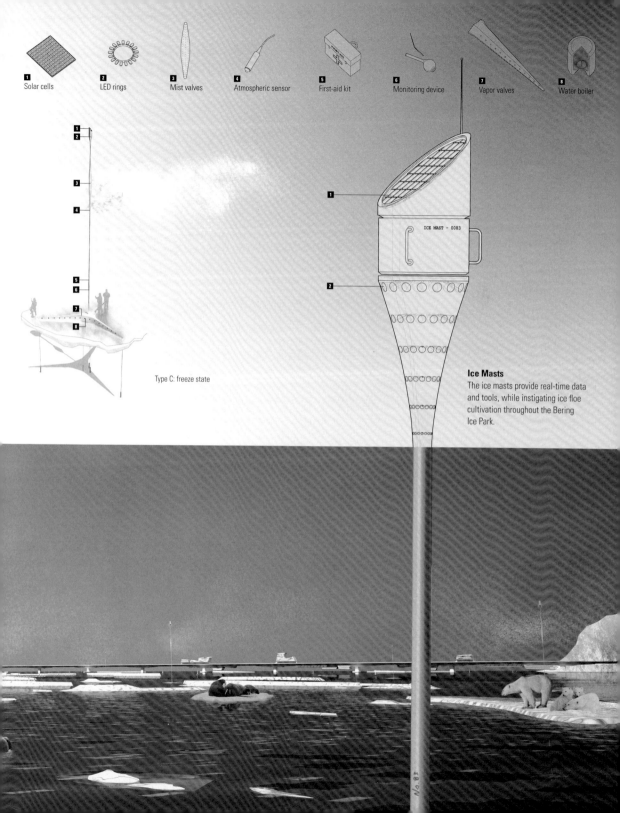

1 Solar cells **2** LED rings **3** Mist valves **4** Atmospheric sensor **5** First-aid kit **6** Monitoring device **7** Vapor valves **8** Water boiler

Type C: freeze state

ICE MAST - 0083

Ice Masts
The ice masts provide real-time data and tools, while instigating ice floe cultivation throughout the Bering Ice Park.

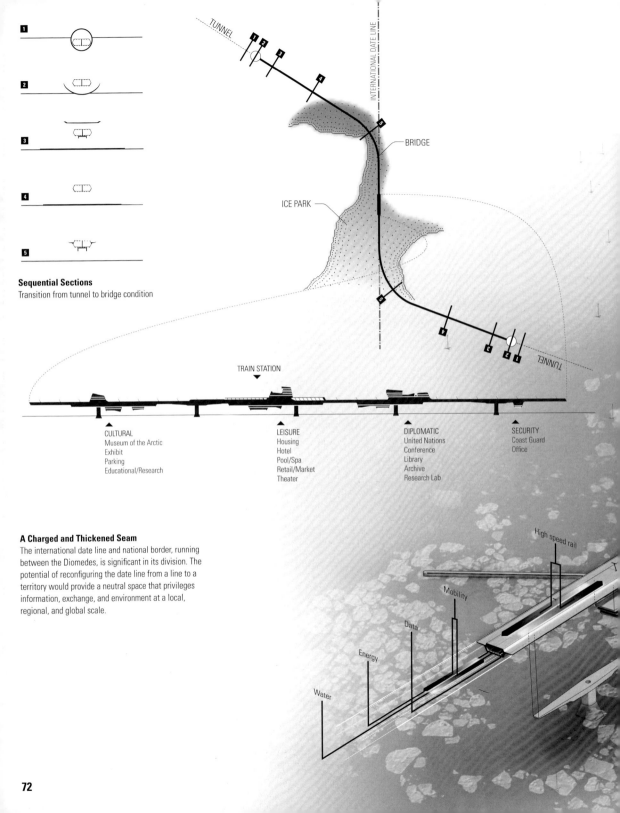

1

2

3

4

5

Sequential Sections
Transition from tunnel to bridge condition

TUNNEL

1 **2**

3

4

INTERNATIONAL DATE LINE

5

BRIDGE

ICE PARK

5

4

3 **2** **1**

TUNNEL

TRAIN STATION

CULTURAL
Museum of the Arctic
Exhibit
Parking
Educational/Research

LEISURE
Housing
Hotel
Pool/Spa
Retail/Market
Theater

DIPLOMATIC
United Nations
Conference
Library
Archive
Research Lab

SECURITY
Coast Guard
Office

A Charged and Thickened Seam
The international date line and national border, running
between the Diomedes, is significant in its division. The
potential of reconfiguring the date line from a line to a
territory would provide a neutral space that privileges
information, exchange, and environment at a local,
regional, and global scale.

High speed rail

Mobility

Data

Energy

Water

Ice-harvesting arm

Water bank piers

Water

Water

Water

Water

A

B

C

A

B

C

Thick Infrastructure

Programs are organized along the IceLink rail/road infrastructure when it is concurrent with the international date line. Public and cultural programs intermittently rise above the bridge, while research and education programs hang below the rail/road. Significant programs include new United Nations headquarters, World Water Council headquarters, the Museum of the Arctic, and extensive oceanographic and meteorological facilities.

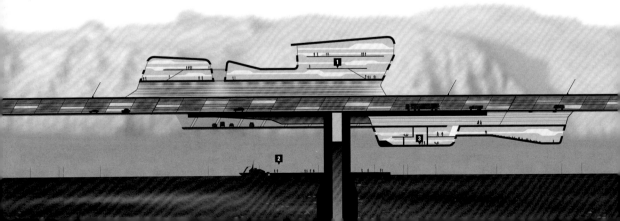

ICE PARK ▶
ENTRANCE 75M

◀ UNITED NATIONS
ENTRANCE 100M
◀ MUSEUM OF THE ARCTIC
ENTRANCE 250M

16km

Programs along the date line
1. Hotel
2. Park access pier
3. Ecology research office space
4. Roadway tunnel
5. Parking
6. High-speed rail station
7. Swimming pool
8. Environment research office space

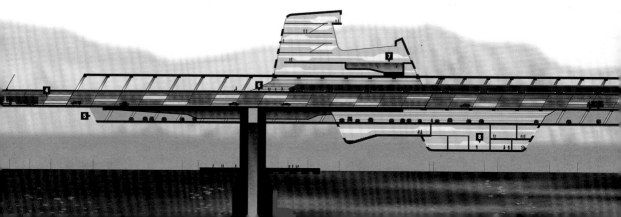

AFTERWORD: FIGURING IT OUT

Christopher Hight

Our present is characterized by simultaneously diffusing disciplinary borders and demands for new specialization. Far from disruptive, such concomitant blurring and delineation has produced and reconstructed architecture as a discipline. How many of Vitruvius's Ten Books would we redact to decouple the canon of European architecture from urbanism and ecology? Is it possible to understand the Maison Domino without the Ville Radieuse? Or even Mies without the Siedlung?

As Manfredo Tafuri and many others have detailed, modernist architecture required the delayed project of the utopian city. Perhaps the origin of this modern coupling could be located by Giambattista Nolli's mid-eighteenth-century map, not only because it portrayed Rome as an ideal site, or because it literally coupled the interior of monumental architecture to urban fabric in a continuous lattice, but because its figure-field visualized what Hannah Arendt would later describe as the dialectic between the *polis* (city) and *oikos* (household) across which modern humanism figured its subjects and regimes of power.[1] To extend her thesis and that of Girogio Agamben's *The Open: Man and Animal* (2002), we might understand the coupling of architecture and the city as an infrastructure for delineating the modern humanist subject. The

architectural project joined to urban program produced signs of apparent intelligibility and recognition—figures of the *anthropos*—within the inhumane dynamics of modernity.

Because such coupling is based on a representational dialectic (which often does not really have two terms but rather one dominate model and a copy), it sublimates the infrastructural geometries necessary for the administration of unprecedentedly large and dense populations of the modern city. When modernists such as Le Corbusier and Ludwig Hilberseimer valiantly attempted to reintroduce infrastructure as guiding logics, they often either decoupled architectural figures from urbanism fields or collapsed the latter into the former as an architectural project itself. In the aftermath of their apparent failure, alternatives were often sought not by narrowing the scope of architectural thought, but by doubling down on the coupling of architecture and urbanism. The results were books and architectural projects that posited architectural practice as research: *Architecture of the City* (Aldo Rossi, 1966), *Learning from Las Vegas* (Robert Venturi, Denise Scott Brown, Steve Izenour, 1972), *Collage City* (Colin Rowe, Fred Koetter, 1978), and *Delirious New York* (Rem Koolhaas, 1978). These either explicitly supplemented Nolli's architecture-urban gestalt (collage), introduced infrastructure as shades of gray (Las Vegas parking lots and signs), or subverted it with narratives that transgressed the border of ink and paper (an athletic club's interior urbanism). What linked them was an attempt to recalibrate architecture and its methods of legibility as an intelligible representation of the chaotic systems and orders of late-capital.

Today, the city, or even urbanism, may no longer serve as architecture's partner in the same way. The dominant forms of power of the late-eighteenth- to mid-twentieth-century city were calibrated to the scale and mode of architectural representation, which in turn provided a productive apparatus for the institutions of a disciplinary state and its collective publics. Biopolitical control operates at scales at once more vastly diffused and intensively molecular than the coupling of architecture-urbanism. Thus, the clearest recent attempt at a disciplinary realignment, landscape urbanism, was first positioned to manage the toxic urban voids left in the wake of capital. Once the site for the production of the subject, the city has become a site for the *anthropos* under erasure.

The projects in this book point to a different response, one that seeks to reposition design as the *figural construction* of new political, technical, and subjective facts outside the debris of the city and modernist dialectics.[2] Translating Gilles Deleuze's articulation of the figural in painting into architecture, the concept can be distinguished from Nolli's figure-ground gestalts in that it is not the construction of sensible representations of meaning, but rather the bringing forth of new facts by relating the sensible and material. The initial list of couplings could be extended to the contemporary condition through Deleuze's questions:

Is there not another type of relationship between Figures, one that would not be narrative, and from which no figuration would follow? Diverse Figures that would spring from the same fact . . . non-narrative relationships between Figures, and non-illustrative relationships between the Figures and Fact? . . . What is this other type of relationship, a relationship between coupled and distinct Figures? Let us call these new relationships matters of fact, as opposed to intelligible relations (of objects or ideas).[3]

This non-illustrative instantiation of matters of fact is what seems to be at stake in the change David Gissen detects in his essay as shifting architecture's relationship from the city to geography, in Keller Easterling's call to make action form, or indeed in InfraNet Lab / Lateral Office's reworking of Rosalind Krauss's diagram as a map of a non-dialectical field of coupled relationships. The latter includes infrastructure as one of four principle material conditions out of which precipitate a field of relations between disciplinary identities. While so-called "infrastructural urbanism" de-emphasizes form (thus replaying the dialectic between intelligible representations and process of operation—chose your dominant term), the possibility here is an architecture that at once stems from and further produces the figural. Indeed, the use of Krauss suggests a renewed commitment to the "art" of architecture. Notably, architecture is removed as a node in this matrix not to erase it but to manifest three latent potential for architecture in the contemporary environment. Far from a passive frame populated with discrete architectural figures, this expanded infrastructural field produces: three figurations of practice hotwiring urbanism and landscape and infrastructure; three configurations of the architect as public agent, manager of forces, and provocateur; and three genre of projects, the programmed container, the productive surface, and the civic conduit.

The figural in architecture could revitalize the field's agency as an anthropomorphic machine, but one finally purged of lingering anthropocentrism. This might seem paradoxical, but as French sociologist Bruno Latour argues, the anthropomorphic should itself be understood not as a center, but as a mediator of couplings, the intermediary between "matters of fact" and political "matters of concern."[4] This sense of *anthropos* is not a fixed figure etched into sand but a figurer, what Latour has called "a weaver of morphisms."[5] The expanded field of relations situates design as neither requiring an intelligible alibi nor determents, but as the political figuration of "matters of fact" that would otherwise not be sensible to the collective subject that it at once articulates and addresses. We should not think of coupling as the singular relation between two terms, culture and nature, architecture and the city, one of which dominates the other as in all dialectics, but as a multiple plural. Not one faithful coupling but promiscuous couplings out of which new forms arise.

Of course, the figural requires more detailed translation into the terms and practices of architectural thought. Indeed, it is likely only a prop or a catalyst that should be dispensed with once the project can be articulated within the field. The reconfigured field outlined here is a disciplinary project for this generation to figure out.

Christopher Hight is an Associate Professor of Architecture and Director of Undergraduate Studies at Rice University School of Architecture.

1. Hannah Arendt, *The Human Condition* (Chicago: University of Chicago Press, 1958).

2. Gilles Deleuze, *Francis Bacon: Logic of Sensation* (Minneapolis: University of Minnesota Press, 2003). This concept of the figural formulated in Deleuze's *Francis Bacon* had a brief architectural moment in the mid-1990s via John Rajchman but was limited by the East Coast formalism to which it was applied.

3. Ibid., 3.

4. Bruno Latour, *What Is the Style of Matters of Concern* (Amsterdam: University of Amsterdam, 2005), 39.

5. Bruno Latour, *We Have Never Been Modern* (Cambridge, MA: Harvard University Press, 1993), 137.

ACKNOWLEDGMENTS

We would like to thank the following institutions for providing forums in which to incubate this work: University of Toronto, University of Waterloo, MIT, Harvard Graduate School of Design, Ohio State University, McGill University, and Virginia Tech; in addition, Planning and Building Department—City of Reykjavík, Canada Council for the Arts, and cityLAB/UCLA.

We would like to thank the following individuals for support, inspiration, and shared dialogue: Ariana Andrei, Javier Arbona, Gaby Aviad, Mark Baechler, George Baird, Philip Beesley, Pierre Bélanger, Tom Bessai, Juhie Bhatia, Vinod and Veena Bhatia, Adrian Blackwell, Anne Bordeleau, Sinisha Brdar, Ricardo Castro, Joshua Cohen, Dana Cuff, Maria Denegri, Alexander D'Hooghe, Kelly Doran, Keller Easterling, Rodolphe El-Khoury, Nathan Freise, Rania Ghosn, Eva Franch Gilabert, David Gissen, Rick Haldenby, Christopher Hight, Robert Levit, David Lieberman, An Te Liu, Mary-Lou Lobsinger, Clare Lyster, Geoff Manaugh, Liat Margolis, Bruce Mau, Jürgen Mayer H., John McMinn, Ann Pendleton-Jullian, Paul Petrunia, Teresa Przybylski, Dereck Revington, Colin Ripley, Christoforos Romanos, Val Rynnimeri, Adrian Sheppard, Sylvia Sheppard, Brigitte Shim, Steve Thompson, Geoffrey Thün, Alexander Trevi, Neyran Turan, Kazys Varnelis, Kathy Velikov, Charles Waldheim, Jane Wolff, Judy and Gilbert White, Lucas White, Zoë White.

PROJECT CREDITS

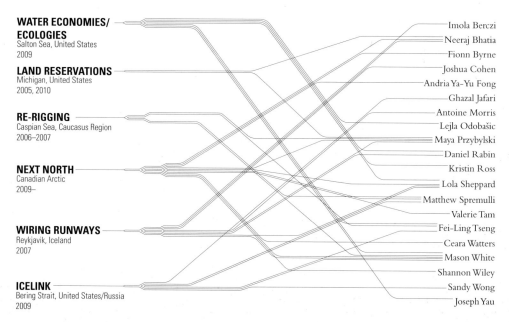

WATER ECONOMIES/ ECOLOGIES
Salton Sea, United States
2009

LAND RESERVATIONS
Michigan, United States
2005, 2010

RE-RIGGING
Caspian Sea, Caucasus Region
2006–2007

NEXT NORTH
Canadian Arctic
2009–

WIRING RUNWAYS
Reykjavik, Iceland
2007

ICELINK
Bering Strait, United States/Russia
2009

Imola Berczi
Neeraj Bhatia
Fionn Byrne
Joshua Cohen
Andria Ya-Yu Fong
Ghazal Jafari
Antoine Morris
Lejla Odobašic
Maya Przybylski
Daniel Rabin
Kristin Ross
Lola Sheppard
Matthew Spremulli
Valerie Tam
Fei-Ling Tseng
Ceara Watters
Mason White
Shannon Wiley
Sandy Wong
Joseph Yau

Pamphlet Architecture was initiated in 1977 as an independent vehicle to criticize, question, and exchange views. Each issue is assembled by an individual author/architect. For information, Pamphlet proposals, or contributions, please write to: Pamphlet Architecture, c/o Princeton Architectural Press, 37 East 7th Street, New York, NY 10003, or go to www.pamphletarchitecture.org.

★ out of print, available only in the collection *Pamphlet Architecture 1–10.*